Which foods are 'natural'?
How can I avoid undesirable additi
How can I convert my family to na
Where do I shop for health foods?
Can my supermarket provide the right foods?
Which pots and pans are best?

Here is a clear and concise introduction to natural foods
– foods free from artificial colouring, preservatives and
other additives. Beatrice Trum Hunter shows how you
can buy and cook natural foods and explains why it is
important to make them the basis of the family's diet.
With the help of this book, you can begin to enjoy a
nourishing, satisfying and healthy diet.

'There is no more practised hand to guide the beginner
through the natural foods jungle.'

The Vegetarian

'For those seriously intending to adopt healthfood
principles. Makes it sound not just easy but positively
inviting.'

The Times

THE NATURAL FOODS PRIMER

The Natural Foods Primer

Help for the Bewildered Beginner

BEATRICE TRUM HUNTER

English edition prepared by Maurice Hanssen

London
UNWIN PAPERBACKS
Boston   Sydney

First published in Great Britain by George Allen & Unwin 1973
First published in Unwin Paperbacks 1979

®
UNWIN PAPERBACKS
40 Museum Street, London WC1A 1LU

British Library Cataloguing in Publication Data

Hunter, Beatrice Trum
    Natural foods primer,
    1. Food, Natural
    I. Title   II, Hanssen, Maurice
    641.3   TX369

    ISBN 0-04-641035-X

Printed in Great Britain by
Hunt Barnard Printing Ltd, Aylesbury, Bucks.

To John

Foreword

Beatrice Trum Hunter has written what I believe to be the first really practical guide for the newcomer to Natural Foods. Too often initial enthusiasm is destroyed because the new style of eating is not enjoyed by the family. This book, the result of a successful personal experience, will guide you cheerfully through the period of dietary change.

It can cost £200,000 to test a new food additive for safety. A relatively small proportion of the three thousand or so additives used in foods in Britain have been tested with the rigour demanded today. This book allows you to positively enjoy good eating without additives and without denatured, over-refined foods.

I hope that this English edition will enable many more families to enjoy the rich and vital life that goes hand in hand with sound nutrition.

MAURICE HANSSEN
President, British Health Food Manufacturers' Association

Contents

Your new style in eating

Are you a newcomer to the idea of natural foods? If you are, welcome to the rapidly expanding club! You probably joined up because you were alarmed by many stories in the news. Although it was reported that mercury-contaminated fish was seized, you were assured that it was 'perfectly safe to eat'. Yet pregnant women were warned against it. Then, there was the cyclamate affair. The safety of this artificial sweetener was cleared several times, but ultimately it was banned. Officials of the US Department of Agriculture have admitted that cancerous organs of meat are cut out, while the rest of the carcass passes inspection. The same agency was willing to allow chickens with a cancer virus to be sold on the market, provided the birds 'do not look too repugnant'. This agency considers pesticide contamination of food 'no imminent hazard' – that is, the food is safe if you don't drop dead five minutes after eating it.

Recent news items may have made you distrustful of repeated assurances that our foods are nourishing. You may recall the one about the rats that were fed white bread and how the animals starved to death because of a dearth of vital nutrients. This evidence fortified the recent testimony that most breakfast cereals are so low nutritionally that they constitute a threat of 'empty calories'. Nutrition surveys have shown disturbing dietary deficiences, affecting not just the poor but also the middle class and the affluent. How can this happen if our foods are nourishing?

Or maybe you have joined the revolt against many of the tasteless, overprocessed fabrications that now pass for food. You have become a label reader and are shocked to find that many present-day foodstuffs seem to be more appropriate for a chemical laboratory than a kitchen. Possibly you are hip, anti-Establishment, and, *Man!* natural foods are the in thing! Or you have long felt a dragged-down, knocked-out feeling of chronic fatigue, and some energetic friend has suggested that improved eating habits may make you feel better.

Whatever your reasons, as a novice you probably have lots of unanswered questions about natural foods. How do you begin? What changes will you have to make in your marketing habits? Where will you find natural foods? Aren't they costly? What changes will you have to make in your meal planning? Doesn't it take more time to prepare natural foods? What kitchen utensils and equipment will you need? If you are an experienced cook, how can you adapt your favourite recipes? How can you substitute more nutritious ingredients and make certain that the rest of your family will not revolt? These are some of the questions beginners ask repeatedly. Many mass-media articles have ridiculed natural food partisans with epithets such as cultists, faddists, crackpots, and a few less kindly. The beginner is apt to think that natural foods consist of concoctions such as marinated seaweed laced with blackstrap molasses and topped with a dollop of yogurt. Not so! Many, if not most of the ingredients, are already known to you. If you are an adventurous cook, you may enjoy experimenting with new ingredients and creating new and better ways of using the old familiar ones.

WHAT IS MEANT BY NATURAL FOODS?

Let's start at the beginning. Aren't all foods natural? The simplest one-sentence definition that I've ever heard was expressed by a housewife, who said, 'The shopper, really informed, and looking for a plain food with nothing added or taken away, is like Diogenes with a lantern unable to find an honest man.'

A food with nothing added? This means that there will be no added preservative, colour, flavour, antioxidant, emulsifier, extender, modifier, bleach, acidifier, clarifier, or any of the other thousands of additives now being used in food processing. It also implies that the food has not been treated with or does not contain any residue of pesticide, hormone, antibiotic, or other chemical, drug or serum that is now commonly used in food production. Nor will the food have unintentional additives, such as transferred wax, phenol, chemical, or other substances from the wrapper or packaging material.

A food with nothing taken away? This means that the food will not be stripped of its essential nutrients, either in the way it is grown, produced, or processed. Produce grown on fertile, well-mineralized soil may be far richer in nutrients than that grown on impoverished soil. Melons, for example, picked unripe, never develop their full mineral, vitamin, or enzyme content, nor do they taste as sweet as those that ripen on the vine. This is also true of other fruits and vegetables. Refining foodstuffs strips them of essential nutrients. If you know what happens in the milling of flour or the refining of sugar, you realize that many vital nutrients are removed or destroyed, and you, the consumer, are short-changed. For this reason you will learn to choose brown rice rather than white, and shun refined sugars.

WHAT WILL NATURAL FOODS DO FOR YOU?

You will discover, or rediscover, the good taste of foods when eaten in their natural state and free of chemicals. Taste a vine-ripened tomato and you'll never again buy the boxed unripe green ones that are merely gassed to redness.

When day by day you eat balanced meals, composed of a variety of foods, you are attempting to supply your body with the necessary nutrients. The rewards of such daily practice should be reflected in a feeling and appearance of well-being, mental alertness, energy, and high resistance to infection. For children especially, good eating habits and wise food selections, started early, may result in lifetime benefits. Natural foods, rich in minerals, vitamins, proteins, enzymes, and other essential elements, help build healthy bodies and promote normal growth for children; an over-consumption of starchy and sugary foods does not.

We have become increasingly aware of the biochemical uniqueness of each individual. Natural foods seem to be 'normalizers' of weight. The elimination of rich sauces and gooey desserts helps trim obese figures, while those painfully thin may lose their gauntness with an improved metabolic balance.

Foods, however, should not be regarded as panaceas. There are no 'miracle foods'. Natural foods should be looked upon as tasty, nourishing, satisfying, and as sensible ingredients in sane life styles.

You're convinced, but how do you convert your family?

Don't be a zealot. If you have become enthusiastic about natural foods but meet with sceptical or even scornful responses from members of your family, go slowly. Drop the subject and avoid discussions that criticize the food habits of others. Your ultimate aim will still be to convert your family, but try to do it gradually, tactfully, and even subtly.

How? Introduce new items in small amounts. If you plan to sneak some brewer's yeast into a vegetable soup, use it sparingly. Put it into the soup when no one is around and don't mention it. As time goes by, you may be able to increase the amount. Or, if you are switching from white bread to whole grain, at first use a half-and-half mixture of 81 per cent extraction rate wholemeal flour, or an unbleached flour, which will taste little different from the bleached stuff. Then increase the proportion of 81 per cent flour until the point is reached at which your family will accept bread made entirely from this flour. The next stage will be to blend the 81 per cent wholemeal with 100 per cent. As you continue, you may reach a point at which your family will accept a bread made with a far greater amount of whole grain than unbleached flour – provided you do it gradually.

When you introduce a new item at the table, where it can be seen by everyone – such as sprouts in the salad – do not announce it with fanfare. If you are questioned, respond, but restrain yourself. Speak enthusiastically about the crisp texture or the sprightly flavour of the sprouts, but refrain from mentioning their vitamin content. Don't join the eat-it-because-it's-so-good-for-you school. This tack is apt to snuff out any spark of interest.

If there are young children in the family, allow them to help you prepare the sprouts, or mix the dough, or roll the biscuits. They are more apt to taste and like foods that they have helped to prepare.

Provide good substitutes. If a dish of sweets has usually been around, replace it with a large bowl of tempting fresh fruit. If soft drinks have been accessible in the refrigerator, substitute some bottles of unsweetened apple juice.

Let your own appearance and vitality convince other members of your family that natural foods are worth trying. When your eyes sparkle, your hair shines, your skin glows, and your mental alertness and energy are obvious, your family will take note. So will relatives, friends, and neighbours. Be prepared to answer questions – such as what to do for a muddy complexion, brittle fingernails, fatigue or weight control. But wait until the questions are asked – as they ultimately will be – and deal with them casually. Before you realize it, those who began scepti-cally and scornfully may outstrip you in their own enthusiasms!

WHAT IF COMPANY IS COMING?

Don't panic when you invite guests who have not yet been exposed to your new style of eating. You will be able to cope with them more easily than you may imagine. Be adaptable and inventive.

If you serve alcoholic drinks before the meal, nurse along one drink for yourself, whatever number your guests may imbibe. Dry wine can be substituted for spirits.* If you have

* Without wishing to be a killjoy, I think that I should state that many wines are now subjected to objectionable processings. Sulphur dioxide, a

virtuously given up alcohol, or have never used the stuff, you can always hold a glass of water in your hand. It looks like vodka. Or you can hold a glass of tomato juice, and your guests may think that you are drinking a Bloody Mary.

Along with the drinks you may want to serve snacks. (Protein foods, eaten with drinks, will buffer the effects of alcohol to some degree.) Instead of the usual salted potato crisps, peanuts, or other items you have discarded from your household, try some wholesome ones:

   carrot strips, green-pepper strips, celery strips, radish roses
   celery filled with herbed cottage cheese or aged natural
      cheese such as Cheddar
   slices of white turnip spread with cottage cheese
   wedges of natural cheeses (pierced with toothpicks)
   raw, unsalted nuts, sunflower or pumpkin seeds

For additional snack suggestions, see page 113. As you continue to entertain, you will improvise. Keep snacks light so that appetites are not dulled.

Remember that your guests may like salad – but don't expect them to eat nearly as much as you have learned to enjoy. Let them help themselves from a large salad bowl. If anyone remarks that salad is 'rabbit food', retort sweetly that it is also 'gorilla food'.

Remember that, judged by your standards, your guests are probably accustomed to eating overcooked vegetables. Steam the vegetables for this meal somewhat longer than is your custom. A small compromise!

Your guests probably expect to have bread on the table. Serve it, by all means, but *you* don't have to indulge. If you think that they will not eat wholegrain bread because they are

toxic substance, is used to prevent oxidative browning. Polyvinylpyrrolidone is frequently used as a clarifier with white wines. Most domestic beer is heavily chemicalized. Soft drinks and mixes, as well as spirits can be a strain on the human liver.

2

unaccustomed to it, serve some wholemeal crispbread. These are familiar to everyone.

Keep on hand some ketchup, mustard, or sauce for guests who are apt to request such items. *You* don't have to indulge.

Dessert is probably the main hurdle. I find that the easiest way to satisfy guests *and* my family is to serve two desserts: fresh fruit and biscuits. My family enjoys the fruit, which may not satisfy the sweet tooth of many guests. They will eat it, but don't regard it as dessert unless it comes as filling for a pie or tart. Biscuits can satisfy the guests, and be made of wholesome ingredients. If you serve fresh fruit and biscuits, you can bypass the biscuit platter.

If your guests expect coffee or tea, by all means serve it. Join them if you wish, but limit yourself to a small amount. Or, if you have virtuously given up such beverages, serve decaffeinated coffee or herb tea. At present many persons – not necessarily natural food consumers – drink decaffeinated coffee.* Often people are curious to try herb teas, especially if they learn that such beverages will not keep them awake at night.

If your guests wish to try herb teas, let them sample peppermint as a starter. This tea has a bracing fragrance, and is usually favoured by novices. Dandelion coffee is another favourite.

You have reached the end of the meal painlessly. You have done your part to have animated conversation on many topics, but you have studiously avoided the subject of natural foods. In a subtle way, more than either you or your guests may appreciate, they have been gently exposed to your new style. Since you have not pressured them, they'll be happy to come again.

INVITED OUT FOR DINNER?

The return visit places you in a more difficult position. Refusal to eat foods may call for an explanation or apology. Excessively

* Although the objectionable caffeine has been removed in decaffeinated coffee, the solvents used for this purpose are also undesirable.

sensitive friends can end up with hurt feelings. In accepting an invitation, remind your hostess or host that you don't indulge in pastas or rich desserts. Say that fresh fruit for dessert will be fine. Add that you are happy that such a dessert will simplify meal planning and preparation. That remark is actually a subtle bit of propaganda for natural foods.

Resist the bread or rolls. Pass up the gravy boat. Shun the biscuits. Chances are that you will still wind up eating certain foods or sauces that you usually avoid. There is also a possibility that the next day you may not feel as well as you generally do after eating your own food at home. Be of good cheer. The point, now reinforced, is that natural foods, well prepared, *do* taste better and make you feel better than those served in a typical way in an average home. An occasional evening out will not matter. It is the day-by-day practice that counts.

PLANNING TO EAT OUT?

You may be fortunate and live in an area where restaurants serve organic or natural foods. Such places are no longer as rare as they used to be. The field is rapidly expanding. A columnist has predicted that in the 1970s natural foods will become the most dynamically expanding segment of the food industry, with such foods available in hotels, restaurants, roadside stands, and on aeroplanes, as well as at other public places where food is served.

But what do you do if such food services are not yet available where you live? A moderately priced restaurant is still a better choice than either a 'greasy spoon' quick-service place or an elegant, expensive restaurant. The quick-service one serves mainly fried items or soggy foods, held all day on a steam table. The expensive restaurant, having a huge menu, rich sauces, oversalted foods, and many frozen items prepared elsewhere and quickly thawed and heated in a microwave oven, does not offer wise choices. Needless to say, much of the price goes for décor, atmosphere, service, and a well-appointed table.

A moderately priced restaurant may have a limited menu, which can be an advantage. The items are more apt to be fresh if the choice is limited. Look at the 'specials' for the day. They will probably be fresher than the printed, standard ones. However, even the 'specials' may not be fresh if they are left-overs. So avoid croquettes, meat loaves, and casseroles, which – as any experienced cook knows – may consist of accumulated bits left from the last few days served in disguised form.

Sometimes seafood restaurants are good choices. Fresh seafoods, cooked to order, plus large salads, are their main-stays. Beverages and desserts may not necessarily be part of the regular menu.

In any restaurant you may do best if you can order *à la carte*. Choose wisely. If the menu has only set dinner prices, make the best selections possible. Here are a few suggestions.

Appetizer   Choose a vegetable or fruit juice, such as tomato or apple. Shun the soups, which are apt to be too salty, thickened with white flour, or filled with pastas or white rice.

Salad   Request oil and vinegar, or a lemon wedge, for the dressing, and prepare it at the table. Smell the oil in the cruet before you pour it, since much restaurant oil is allowed to stand at room temperature and becomes rancid. If the oil has an objectionable odour, just use the vinegar or lemon. Shun the ready-made dressings, which may contain several objection-able chemical additives.

Entrée   You may find items on the menu such as grilled or baked fish, roast beef, grilled steak or lamb chops, roast lamb, roast chicken, turkey, or duck. Try to order fish in season. It is more likely to be fresh. If you can't get roast beef served with its own juices, request that the gravy be left off. Make the same request with roast lamb. If you order fowl, request that the gravy, stuffing, and sweetened cranberry jelly be omitted. If your meat is accompanied by toast or fried bread, leave the bread on the plate.

Vegetables Assume that they are canned or frozen and are overcooked. Sometimes you can order a double portion of salad instead of the vegetable. If you have a choice of potatoes, try to get a baked one. Do not select mashed potatoes, which are apt to be reconstituted, instant, and loaded with chemical additives. Do not select fried potatoes, which most likely are fried in reheated oil of poor quality. If the choice is limited solely to mashed or fried potatoes, try to substitute another vegetable for the potato.

Bread and Rolls Shun the basket.

Dessert Raw fruits rarely appear on menus in restaurants. Sometimes you can order half a grapefruit at the start or the end of a meal. Remove the inevitable maraschino cherry garnish before eating the fruit. 'Melon in season' may be listed, but, alas, it generally happens to be out of season for the restaurant, despite the fact that melons may be abundantly available at markets at the time. Sometimes 'fresh fruit salad' is listed among the desserts on the menu, or it may appear among the appetizers. As you know, this is usually a combination of mainly canned fruit with a few pieces of raw fruit. Leave the maraschino cherries, as well as the juice – which is apt to be a sugary syrup – at the bottom of the dish. Occasionally you can get stewed fruit. Shun the juice, which is also likely to be a sugary syrup. You can rinse off the syrup from individual pieces of fruit by dipping them in your water glass with a teaspoon.

If one must dine out frequently, there are many discouragements. To overcome them, I suggest the following. Plan to carry from home a few items that will supplement restaurant fare. A woman can carry them in her handbag, and a man can carry them in a suit pocket. For example, if you enjoy eating bread with your meal, take a slice or two of your own good bread in a plastic bag, and slip it out unobtrusively. If you enjoy fresh fruit at the end of a meal, carry an orange, tangerine, or apple. These are easy to handle. If you are too embarrassed to eat the fruit while still in the restaurant, eat it after you leave. If you prefer herb tea to other beverages, carry a herb tea bag. Order a cup of boiling water and calmly lower you tea bag into it, allow to infuse for a minute or so and enjoy your preferred drink.

TAKING YOUR LUNCH TO WORK?

You can have an adequate and varied lunch by planning to take some goodies from home. Choose from the following. They are easy to clean and cut, can be wrapped the night before and refrigerated until you leave home in the morning.

Salads Choose items that you can eat by hand, without dressing. If you wish, keep a shaker of sea-salt at your place of work and use it for seasoning. Choose raw pieces of celery, carrots, green peppers, white or yellow turnips, cucumbers, cauliflower, or courgettes. Or choose whole tomatoes or radishes. Or carry a plastic bag of sprouts, sprigs of parsley or watercress, leaves of any variety of lettuce, or wedges of green or red savoy.

Protein You will not have to face sandwich lunches day after day. Vary with hard-boiled, herbed eggs, or devilled eggs; a wedge of a natural hard cheese; cooked sliced roast beef, chicken, turkey, or duck; a small container of cottage cheese, cashew, or peanut butter; sunflower or pumpkin seeds; raw nuts; a small can of sardines, tuna fish, or salmon. For these foods, keep a spoon and fork at your place of work. Refrigerate such foods, if possible, in warm weather.

Fruits Choose those that are easy to handle, such as grapes, an orange, tangerine, apple, pear, banana, peach, or dried fruits. Keep a knife handy at your place of work.

Beverage If you can transport a squat, wide-mouthed Thermos easily, fill it with something to drink. In hot weather this might be unsweetened fruit juice, tomato juice, milk, or yogurt. In cold weather you might enjoy the warmth of home-made soup or herb tea. If you don't find it convenient to carry a Thermos, you can have on hand a supply of small cans with individual servings of fruit juices or tomato juice. Half and quarter pint containers of yogurt are available, but when buying be sure to read the listed ingredients and avoid those brands which use artificials.

If you take your lunch to work, you will find that you can eat very well – and save money too. Many of these suggestions are also good for picnicking and car travel.

HAVING A QUICK SNACK?

When you are pressed for time, on the run, or in need of a quick pick-up, what can you order?

Items to Choose	*Items to Omit or Avoid*
open sandwich of roast beef, sliced chicken, turkey, egg, tuna fish, salmon, sardines, liver paste; accompanied by cole slaw, lettuce and tomato, or potato salad	garnishes of sauces, pickles, olives; mayonnaise, gravy, potato crisps. If the sandwich is closed, at least discard the top slice of bread
cottage cheese, unprocessed English and Continental cheeses	some restaurants use processed, Cheddar-type cheeses
tomato juice, vegetable juice, pineapple juice, unsweetened apple, grape, or cranberry juice, milk, or yogurt	soft drinks, cola drinks, imitation fruit drinks, soda, chocolate milk
whole wheat toast, butter, bowl of soup, stewed fruit	jam or jelly, biscuits, pastries, pies, cakes, doughnuts, ice cream, Danish pastries, sweets

As you will soon realize, you will constantly be faced with choices. Those you make can be wise or unwise. They can build a sense of well-being or fatigue. They can lead to health or disease.

How do you shop?

If you are a beginner and feel bewildered, take heart! Start right where you are. Go slowly, and gradually you will become knowledgeable. The chances are that you have been shopping in your local supermarket. So start in your supermarket and see what you can find.

If your supermarket is typical, you are confronted with a staggering array of items. Faced with this variety, you have found that shopping is bewildering. Decisions! DECISIONS! DECISIONS! Once you have mastered a few basic facts about natural foods, you will find that supermarket shopping is simplified. By making *wise choices* you will learn to walk right past certain aisles and limit your selections to a few areas.

Plan to spend an hour on an educational tour of your supermarket. You will find it both entertaining and enlightening. Read as many labels as you can on packaged items. If you use reading glasses, take them along. You might also take a strong magnifying lens, which may be necessary to read some of the small type. You may have to turn packages around to find the listing of ingredients, but persist. Be sure to read the label ingredients for the following: imitation orange-juice drinks, instant mashed potatoes, convenience and slimming foods, processed cheeses, and packaged dry breakfast cereals.

On your tour play this little game. Determine *not* to place any food in your shopping basket that includes any of the following on the label:

Artificial colour or flavour
Preservative, such as sulphur dioxide or sodium benzoate

Sodium nitrate or sodium nitrite

Flavour enhancer, such as monosodium glutamate (MSG), disodium inosinates, or guanylates

Freshness preserver (antioxidant, oxygen interceptor) such as BHA (butylated hydroxyanisole), BHT (butylated hydroxytoluene), propyl gallate, or NDGA (nordihydro-guaiaretic acid)

Mould retarder, such as sodium propionate or calcium propionate

Emulsifier, such as monoglyceride or diglyceride

Thickening agent, such as sodium carboxymethylcellulose

Bleach, such as chlorine dioxide in flour

Hydrogenated fat (or partially hydrogenated, hardened, or partially hardened)

Refined sugar (sucrose, dextrose, glucose, corn syrup, brown sugar)

Artificial sweetener (saccharin)

Any other long chemical term, unfamiliar to you, that would require being checked in a technical reference book

What is left, you may ask? Plenty! You will discover that what you have shunned are the excessively processed fabricated foods; what you have selected are the basic ones. This will mean that you will be preparing meals 'from scratch' and that *you* will control the quality. If you have paid close attention to the above list, your shopping tour might end up somewhat as follows:

Items I Have Chosen	*Items I Have Avoided*
fresh meats	luncheon meats, frankfurters
fresh fish	frozen fish fingers
butter	margarine
cream	non-dairy creamer
natural hard cheese, cottage cheese	processed cheese
fresh cherries	maraschino cherries
fresh lemons	reconstituted lemon juice
fresh oranges	orange drink

Items I Have Chosen—continued	*Items I Have Avoided—continued*
fresh milk, yogurt, buttermilk	milk substitute
bag of potatoes	instant mashed potatoes
fresh peas in the pod	canned green peas
fresh blackberries	blackberry tarts
fresh peaches	canned peaches in heavy syrup
100% pure olive oil	refined vegetable oil
canned fruit juice, unsweetened	canned fruit drink, sweetened
fresh apples	apple pie
bottled tomato juice	bottled soft drinks
100% pure maple syrup	imitation maple syrup
100% pure honey	refined white sugar
unsulphured molasses	sulphured molasses
package of nuts in the shell	package of salted, roasted nuts
fresh coconut	package of sweetened coconut shreds
sun-dried raisins	golden seedless raisins with sulphur dioxide
unbleached white flour, whole wheat flour, stoneground whole-meal flour, 81%; rye flour	bleached, bromated white flour
whole wheat bread	white bread
brown rice	white rice
wheat germ, porridge oats (not instant), cracked wheat or oatmeal to be cooked	packaged dry breakfast cereal ready to eat
poultry	frozen chicken pie
eggs	fancy cake mixes
pure vanilla extract	vanillin

As you can see, even the supermarket offers plenty of wise choices. You will note that most of your purchases are from the produce department and the sections where you can find fresh meat, poultry, fish, eggs, and dairy products.

If you are accustomed to keeping spare food on hand, there are a few processed items that are not highly objectionable. Use them with discretion as occasional choices rather than on a daily basis. These include items such as canned stewed tomatoes; cans or jars of tomato juice; canned or frozen unsweetened fruit juices; canned water-packed fruit; canned sardines; canned salmon; canned or frozen vegetables without added sugar;* cans or jars of corn on the cob, or of red peppers. Remember that all canned foods have been heated. Certain valuable vitamins and enzymes have been destroyed. Compared to briefly steamed fresh vegetables, canned ones will be overcooked and limp. If you have to reheat them before serving they suffer further loss of nutrients. If you use these processed foods at all, use them sparingly, and do not equate them with fresh foods.

Do you stop here? No, indeed. Just consider this as a first step. You have a daily opportunity to reach for good choices and wean yourself away from junk items. In time you will come to recognize that the so-called 'fresh' produce of the supermarket is still likely to be tainted with pesticide residue. The whole wheat flour, on the shelf for months, has become rancid even though you cannot smell it. The nuts in the shell may have been bleached to make their colour uniform. The butter and natural cheeses may contain artificial colour, without label declaration although cheeses will soon have to state if colour is added. Nevertheless, remember that at the beginning of your conversion, even supermarket food, wisely selected, has started you in a direction of improved nutrition. Although the choices from the supermarket have not eliminated the pesticide problem, they have greatly reduced the number of many unnecessary exposures to chemical additives in your daily food intake.

WHAT IS THE NEXT STEP?

Look for sources of natural foods that have been grown organically. Fruits and vegetables should be grown in fertile soil, be tree- or vine-ripened, and produced without exposure to poisonous pesticides. Meat, poultry, and eggs should be from animals raised in a healthful atmosphere, with access to the

* Read the labels carefully. Canned peas, carrots, and other vegetables when canned frequently have sugar added. This is also true of jars of vegetables intended as baby food.

outdoors, light, sunshine, exercise, and wholesome feed. Fish should be from safe waters. Such foods are obtainable, provided you are willing to exert some effort to find them. You will be willing to make the effort once you are convinced that such foods taste better, are more nourishing, and are safer to eat than those that are more artificially processed and readily accessible.

Depending on your locality, there are different ways to find organic food sources. Suppose that you live in a large city. You may feel that the situation is hopeless, so far removed from farms, orchards, and fields where food is raised. But there are possibilities. Let your fingers do the walking through the yellow pages of the classified telephone directory. Look under the classification 'Health Foods'. Although formerly many of these stores sold only packaged foods, many of them now stock fresh produce, meats, fish, poultry, eggs, dairy products, nuts, seeds, and grains, and have refrigerator and freezer sections.

If you locate a health food store, but find that its stock is limited, don't be discouraged. Speak to the manager and tell him what you would like to buy. He might be willing to stock a limited number of items, such as eggs and produce, if he could be certain that these foods would have a steady sale. If the store lacks a refrigerator or freezer, or if the equipment is too limited, requests from customers such as yourself might encourage the manager to invest in new equipment or expand his facilities to take care of increased consumer demands.

If you fail to find a health food store, what other resources might you tap? Some nationwide chains such as Marks and Spencer are very conscious of the need to provide nutritionally sound foods, though even there you must still check the labels. Many department stores and a few supermarkets have a small health food section. In areas where there is no specialist health food store, although such places become rarer each day, perhaps your supermarket manager could be persuaded to stock the basic items you require.

In one American area members of a Co-op organized an ambitious programme as early as 1958. Some fifty to sixty people formed a sister organization, Organic Food Co-op, Inc. Although the group is independent and has never received financial assistance from the Co-op movement, relationships are cordial. Operations began modestly in the first president's basement, which was used as a store for foodstuffs brought there by volunteer members. The group experienced growing pains by the following year, and larger quarters were rented. A built-in refrigerator and salaried store manager required money. An enterprise of this type inevitably has ups and downs. This one managed to survive the difficult times because of the continuous efforts of volunteers. Many of them had at one time been gravely ill. They considered the store as a lifeline to foods vital for their survival and well-being. At present the shop sells a wide variety of organically grown natural foods. This venture may serve as an example for you.

In the absence of a helpful multiple, where can you turn? Approach an independently owned supermarket or grocery store, preferably one where you shop and are known. Take an inventory of items already stocked there that meet with your approval. (Use the 'Items I Have Chosen' list on pages 28–29 earlier in this chapter.) The list may be small, but commend the manager for stocking the items. Ask him if he would be willing to stock additional foods. Suggest items with long shelf life and those apt to be purchased by other customers as well. These might include cider vinegars or natural fruit and vegetable juices. If you can get the manager's initial co-operation, let him decide how he wants to display these foods. He may decide on a special 'natural foods' section, or prefer to place such items with 'dietary foods', 'gourmet' items, or in a delicatessen section. Or he may decide to place the natural foods on shelves along with the regular stock. For instance, uncooked porridge oats may be placed next to the most instantized ready oats; raw sugar jams may be next to the coloured, refined sugar varieties.

Be mindful of a few points. Choose familiar foodstuffs. If these sell well, gradually introduce more. Give assurance that you will make repeated purchases of the items you request, and point out that others may become interested. Try to involve your friends, family, and neighbours. Be prepared to supply names and addresses of wholesale suppliers of special foods, which by this time you will have acquired. Make use of the 'unique selling points', as advertising experts describe them by suggesting that unsalted tomato ketchup can also be sold to those who seek low-sodium food, or water-packed fruit to those who want sugar-free food.

If your initial efforts succeed, suggest foods that have a relatively long shelf life but are less well known. Among these – once you yourself are more familiar with natural foods – you might request the stocking of seeds for sprouting, agar-agar as a setting agent, unsweetened dried cocunut shreds, herb teas, barley kernels, arrowroot starch, unblended honey, or wheat germ. When your help is needed, supply information. For example, give assurance that crystallized unblended honey has not spoiled. Or suggest ways in which barley kernels can be used, since customers will not buy items if they don't know how to use them. Later you may request the stocking of perishable foods such as fertile eggs, crude vegetable oils, old-fashioned peanut butter, produce, meat and poultry.

There have been some heartening developments. Large supermarket chains have begun, on their own initiative, to stock organic foods for the convenience of interested customers. We know of one in America that has two different types of operations catering to natural food customers. On the first day when fresh produce is delivered to its various stores customers are invited to make bulk purchases directly from the crates. Some purchase twenty-five pounds or more of such foods as carrots. By the day's end most of the organic produce has been sold.

The second operation is self-service buying of packaged produce in the stores. Here's how it is organized. The produce is packaged the same as any other produce handled in the store and is displayed in the same area. However, a special sign is placed over the organic produce and special tags are affixed to the packages. Pertinent information, obtained from the suppliers, is given. This supermarket chain finds that it can sell as much organic food as it can obtain. A similar scheme operates in the Migros stores in Switzerland and in the Neuform health stores in Germany.

In addition to these city sources, ingenious approaches have been devised by individuals eager to obtain organic food through small neighbourhood shops. A friend of mine, for instance, who is fond of sweet potatoes, located a distant organic grower who was willing to ship. But my friend had a problem. A lug, the shipping measure, was too large for her modest living quarters and small family. She approached the owner of a small fruit and vegetable store where she shopped with this proposition: She would order a lug of sweet potatoes and have them shipped to his store if he in turn would be willing to sell her a few pounds and sell the remainder to other customers, with a margin of profit for himself. The man agreed to try the arrangement. The sweet potatoes were ordered, arrived, and were displayed with a sign made by my friend's child: *Organically Grown Sweet Potatoes, Not Artificially Dyed*. The response was surprisingly good. After the original lug was sold quickly and profitably, the owner himself suggested a reorder. A similar approach, used elsewhere, has permitted city dwellers to purchase small quantities of organically grown citrus fruit, papayas, avocados, melons, and other produce usually shipped in quantity.

If you live in the suburbs or country, what additional possibilities exist for getting organic foods? No matter how little land is available to you, some of it can be used to raise some of your own foods – organically, of course. Even with limited space, you can grow a surprising number of vegetables. By careful planning you can intercrop your vegetables and flowers. It may shock your neighbours to see cabbages growing outside your living room window, but who cares? You can even make the same planting space do double duty one season. Plant an early crop such as radishes. After harvesting them, plant another crop. If your land is limited, plant dwarf espalier fruit trees. Make your ornamentals functional as well.

Try to find neighbours who are interested in organic gardening. If you succeed, consider the possibility of swapping surplus harvested crops. Also try to locate organic farms.* Even if you end up driving through the countryside for some distance to locate natural foods, you will become convinced that the effort is worthwhile.

As you become interested in discovering sources for organic food, regardless of where you live, you will find that there are many possibilities. Some are apparent; others take ingenuity. As more people are becoming interested, there are various organized efforts to meet these needs. There is a concerted effort to have organic food tested and certified in order to eliminate fraud in this rapidly expanding field.

Even after you have located sources of organic foods it is unlikely that such items will constitute 100 per cent of your food intake. Very rarely do people achieve this goal, unless they grow most of their own foods or happen to be extremely affluent. Present consumer demand outstrips supply and distribution of some items. You may feel that the higher costs strain your budget. Or you may not find it possible to drive long distances for certain foods.

Just remember that *some* is better than *none*. Whether you are eating 20 per cent, 70 per cent, or 90 per cent of organically raised foods, any effort in this direction is worthwhile. Work towards a goal of increasing your organic intake. Meanwhile supplement whatever organic food you can get with natural food, and eliminate the junk.

* The Soil Association will provide a list of organic growers.

3

What are the basic natural foods?

Of course you are already familiar with many natural foods that are obtainable everywhere. But as you begin to shop in health food stores, special sections of supermarkets, and to look through the catalogues of mail-order suppliers you may encounter some new and unfamiliar items. Here is an alphabetical listing, with some information that will familiarize you with these items and help you decide if you want to try them.

Acerola These are Caribbean cherries that are extremely rich in vitamin C. They are generally dried and prepared in tablet form. See also *rose hips.*

Agar-agar This is a sea vegetable that will thicken juices, similar to gelatin. It contains no animal source. It usually comes as a flake or powder. See also *gelatin.*

Apple cider Obtain this juice unsweetened, without preservatives.

Arrowroot starch This is a natural thickening agent. It can be used instead of white flour.

Baking yeast This is a leavening yeast for breads and baked goods. It can be bought as dry yeast granules in bulk. The granules will be active for at least six months, without refrigeration, if they are stored in a tightly closed jar and kept cool and dry. It is far more economical to buy the granules in bulk rather than by the individual cake or packet, since the major cost of the individual portions results from expensive packaging. If you plan to bake your own bread, the granules can be purchased in quarter-, half-, and one-pound amounts. One rounded dessert-spoon of the yeast granules equals one packet or one square of yeast. One pound of yeast granules equals approximately forty-eight yeast cakes.

Barley Look for the hulled whole grain. Do not buy pearled or polished barley, which has been stripped of some nutrients. The hulled whole grain barley is good in soups, stews, casseroles, or as a rice substitute.

Barley flour The barley grain has been ground. The flour is a flavoursome addition to other flours for baking purposes. Since barley flour does not contain gluten, this flour by itself will not make a dough that will hold together for a satisfactory loaf of bread.

Barley (cracked) Rougher than barley flour. It is good in soups, stews, casseroles, or as a rice substitute.

Bean sprouts Grown from Moong seed, which is available from Indian stores. See pp. 97–98 for sprouting directions.

Blackstrap molasses This is a syrup rich in nutrients, but rather bitter. Use it sparingly and combine it with honey if you find it too strong. Also called *crude* black molasses.

Bran This is the residue after whole wheat flour has been ground and sifted. It is coarse cellulose and provides bulk for those suffering from chronic constipation. It may be too rough for some individuals; a little goes a long way.

Brewer's yeast This is a non-leavening yeast that is a nutritional supplement. It is also known as 'nutritional yeast', 'primary yeast', or 'food yeast'. It is an excellent, inexpensive source of the vitamin B complex, as well as protein. It can be used in many ways by being added to cool or warm water, milk, fruit juices, soups, to batter, casseroles, or baked beans. Since the taste is strong, begin with a small amount. Its flavour can be disguised in dishes with other strong-flavoured ingredients such as molasses. It is sold as a powder or tablet. If you do not find one brand of brewer's yeast palatable, try another. The taste of brewer's yeast varies considerably from brand to brand. By experimenting you will succeed in finding one that pleases you and your family.

Buckwheat Get this whole grain hulled. Sometimes it is toasted, and you will find that this improves the flavour. Use it as cereal or a rice substitute.

Buckwheat flour The buckwheat has been ground and is a flavoursome addition to other flours for baking. See note under *barley flour*, above. Buckwheat flour is a heavy, dark flour. Since the buckwheat is a soft grain, you can grind it easily in small quantities in an electric blender without fear of dulling the blades.

Butter Get freshly churned sweet butter made from sweet cream, and preferably dated. If the date is coded, ask the store manager to decode it. Even better, try to locate butter made from certified raw cream.

Buttermilk This is a familiar item to all. Special therapeutic properties are attributed to it, as well as to other fermented milks, such as kumiss, kefir, and yogurt. The protein precipitate in all these fermented milk products is in the form of a fine curd, which may permit them to be digested more quickly than plain milk.

Carob powder This powder is ground from the carob pod, which comes from a tree in the locust family. Carob powder can be bought either plain or toasted. The latter closely resembles chocolate in flavour, but it has none of the undesirable features of chocolate. Chocolate is high in fat, carob is not. For many people chocolate is an allergen, especially for migraine-headache sufferers; it is unlikely that carob would have such adverse effects. Chocolate contains theobromine, a stimulant similar to caffeine; carob is free of stimulants. Carob is rich in minerals and natural sugars. A great variation exists in the flavour of carob, as well as in the price. Some powders are far more chocolatelike than others. A few are flat and disagreeably gritty. If you fail to find a palatable carob powder the first time you try it, don't despair. Try another brand. Keep experimenting until you find one that you like. Carob powder is also sold as 'carob flour'. Flour is a misnomer, since it is not a flour, ground from grain; it is merely finely ground. Carob is also known as 'St-John's-bread', 'honey locust', 'locust bean', and 'Boecksur'.

Carob syrup A natural sweetener condensed from carob.

Carrageen See *Irish moss.*

Cheeses, hard Buy natural, aged cheeses, preferably those made from raw milk. Some are made without added colour or salt.

Cheeses, soft See *cottage cheese.*

Coconut meal See *coconut shreds.*

Coconut shreds Buy those that are dried and unsweetened, without added glycerin or preservatives. These shreds make festive toppings for fresh fruit salads or can be used in baked goods.

Corn, dried You can purchase dry or parched corn kernels.
They need to be soaked and then cooked before being served
as a vegetable. They are good in soups, stews, or casseroles
when fresh corn is not in season.

Cornell Mix This is a flour mixture, also known as 'triple
rich'. See p. 101 for the Cornell Mix Bread recipe.

Cottage cheese This is a familiar item to all. Make certain that
it is fresh, since it is highly perishable. If coded, rather than
dated, ask the store manager to decode the date.

Cream See the remarks for *cottage cheese*, above.

Dulse This is a seaweed rich in minerals, vitamins, and trace
elements. In Nova Scotia children eat it like sweets. The
dried leaves can be chewed or cut up and used in fish chowders
or seafood casseroles. See also *kelp*.

Eggs Free range eggs are becoming fairly plentiful. By
choosing these you ensure that the hen has had a mixed diet
with good effects on the resultant egg. Deep litter eggs are
produced in surroundings more comfortable to the hen than
battery cages, but not necessarily more nutritious. The Trade
Descriptions Act makes it an offence to sell an egg as 'free
range' unless this is a genuine fact.

Fenugreek seeds These are good for sprouting or as herb tea.
See pp. 97–98 for sprouting directions.

Flavourings Be prepared to spend a little more money and
buy pure extracts instead of the synthetics.

Flours Purchase flour from grains not subjected to fumigants, and those that have been freshly ground, preferably
by stone.

Food yeast See *brewer's yeast.*

Fruit juices The first choice is freshly squeezed, pressed, or extracted unstrained juice from raw fruit, without any sweetening added. If you use canned or frozen juices, read the labels and select those that contain no added sweeteners or preservatives.

Fruits, dried Buy the sun-dried fruits without preservatives such as sulphur dioxide or aids to appearance such as mineral oil. Unfortunately, it is not easy to find natural sun-dried fruits, so it is best to rinse before soaking unless you are sure of the quality. You can eat dried fruits just as they are, or you can soften them by soaking them overnight in cold water or for a few hours in warm water. Soaking eliminates any need to cook them. Use the liquid, which is mineral-rich. Remember that dried fruits are very concentrated in sweetness. Eat them sparingly. There is such a thing as too much of a good thing – even with natural food!

Fruits, fresh Buy tree- or vine-ripened fruits if possible, with the exception of bananas. (See p. 60) Better still, try to get organically produced fruits.

Gelatin Buy the plain, unflavoured, unsweetened gelatin and use it with unsweetened fruit juice and fresh fruit. See also *agar-agar.*

Gluten flour This is an elastic substance, found mainly in wheat and rye flours, that gives adhesiveness to dough. It is formed when the proteins in flour absorb water. Since gluten coagulates when it is heated, it helps to give shape to baked bread. Gluten flour can be added to bread dough. Some people are allergic to gluten flour.

Gruenkern This is dried, unripened green wheat kernels, which can be added to soups, stews, and casseroles.

Honey There is a great variety of honey flavours, depending on what flowers the bees have worked to extract the nectar. The range is from mild, light-coloured clover to strong, dark-coloured buckwheat. Experiment until you find a honey flavour you and your family enjoy. Light-flavoured honey is preferable for baking, so that the honey flavour will not predominate; strong-flavoured honey is good on cereal and toast. Look for the word 'unblended' on the label unless you prefer a particular, specified mixture. If the honey has begun to crystallize, it has not spoiled.

Irish moss This is a seaweed that can be used to thicken desserts such as blancmange. It is also called 'carrageen'. It is an irritant for some people.

Kalamata beans See *moong beans*.

Kelp This is a seaweed rich in minerals, vitamins, and trace elements. It can be bought in granules and powder form and used as a seasoning. It can also be bought in tablet form and used daily as a nutritional supplement. See also *dulse*, above.

Lecithin granules These granules, made from defatted soy-beans, provide a rich source of phosphatides and can be used as a nutritional supplement. The granules can be eaten as they are or sprinkled on cereal, in soup, or mixed with liquid. They are also called 'soy phosphatides'.

Lecithin liquid This is a viscous liquid form of lecithin, which can be mixed with vegetable oils or butter or used in baked goods to add beneficial unsaturated fat to the diet.

Lentils These well-known beans when purchased whole can be used for sprouting. See sprouting directions on pp. 97–98.

Malt This syrup is generally made from germinated barley.

It is good in beverages and baked goods and is less sweet than some other natural sweeteners.

Maple sugar This is maple syrup that has been cooked until it granulates. It resembles light brown sugar in appearance.

Maple syrup Buy 100 per cent pure maple syrup that has been produced without formaldehyde disinfecting pellets.

Meal This is coarse flour, such as cornmeal or rye meal.

Meats Buy fresh meats and have the butcher trim away all visible fat. Have meat minced freshly to your order, and watch it being minced in your presence. Even better, try to locate fresh or frozen meat from producers who do not use feed concentrates, hormones, or tranquillizers for their livestock.

Milk If you use milk, get fresh whole or skim milk. Even better, try to get certified raw milk. If you use milk powder, buy the kind processed with low-heat spray, not high-heat roller. Since this information is not usually on the label, write to the processor and find out which method has been used. (Also see footnote, p. 91.)

Millet This is a whole grain, widely used for centuries in the Far East. The grain is good in soups, stews, casseroles, or as a rice substitute.

Millet flour The millet has been ground, and it is a good addition to other flours for baking purposes. See note under *barley flour*, above.

Molasses Buy dark, unsulphured molasses. See also *blackstrap molasses*.

Moong or mung beans These are dry beans that can either be cooked or sprouted. For sprouting directions, see pp. 97–98.

In Greek neighbourhoods these beans are known as 'Kalamata beans'.

Natural sweeteners   See *blackstrap molasses, raw sugar, honey, malt, maple syrup, molasses.*

Natural thickeners   See *agar-agar, arrowroot starch, gelatin, potato starch, tapioca starch, unbleached flour.*

Nutritional yeast   See *brewer's yeast.*

Nuts   Buy raw nuts, in the shell, or nuts that are raw, unsalted, unoiled, and without antioxidant, packed in vacuum tins.

Oat flour   This flour, made from ground oats, makes baked goods light and fine-textured.

Oatmeal   This popular breakfast-cereal comes in two different forms. One is steel-cut and is known as 'Irish oatmeal' or 'Scotch oatmeal'. It consists of hard pieces of cracked oats, or oat groats, and requires cooking. The other is rolled oats, the flattened flakes that can be eaten raw if combined with liquid, or lightly cooked. Use the rolled oats for making biscuits or bread, and use the steel-cut oats for porridge.

Oats   This is a whole grain that can be cooked or sprouted. The hulls tend to cling to the grains, but will float on top of the water when the grain is cooked. Then the hulls can be skimmed off.

Oils   There is a wide variety of vegetable oils from which you can make your selections. They should be sold in dark bottles or tins. Buy oils in small quantities, and plan to use them promptly. You can choose from the following vegetable oils: corn, olive, peanut, safflower, sesame, soybean, or sunflower. Others, not as commonly found, include almond, apricot kernel, avocado, and walnut. Sometimes oils are sold mixed, so that you get all the essential fatty acids (EFA) vital for bodily functions and good health. Three essential fatty acids (linoleic, linolenic, and arachidonic) are found in many vegetable oils that are high in unsaturated fats. Perhaps a few words of explanation are necessary, since advertising and hucksterism have left the public in a state of confusion.

A fat is distinguished from an oil by its physical consistency. At room temperature, if solid, it is considered a fat; if liquid, an oil. In the natural state, however, either fat or oil can gradually revert to liquid or solid by having the temperature raised or lowered. The characteristic solidity or liquidity depends, generally, on the degree of saturation of the fatty acids. The more solid they are, the higher the saturation; the fluid oils are nearly all unsaturated to some degree. In general, vegetable oils are highly unsaturated, while animal fats are highly saturated. (There are exceptions. For example, coconut oil, a vegetable fat, is highly saturated; fish oil, an animal fat, is highly unsaturated.)

Since the unsaturates contain the highly desirable EFA, which vegetable oils should you choose? The answer to this depends upon your personal taste, since some of the oils are strong, while others are mild. It also depends on your budget, since prices vary. Additionally, you can be guided by the various amounts of unsaturated fatty acids and saturated ones that the different oils contain, in order to make a wise nutritional selection. The US Department of Agriculture lists the following fatty-acid content of oils, measured in grams per 100 grams ether extract or crude fat:

Oil	Unsaturated Fatty Acids	Saturated Fatty Acids
corn	84	10
olive	84	11
peanut	76	18
safflower	87	8
sesame	80	14
soybean	80	15
sunflower	83	12

Although cottonseed oil is also high in unsaturates and relatively low in saturates, it is best avoided for reasons discussed on page 52. Coconut oil should also be shunned, since it is the one liquid oil that is highly saturated.

What does the term 'cold-pressed' mean for vegetable oil? Actually the term is meaningless. Even when the hydraulic and screwtype presses are used, only the first few drops of oil pressed out are truly cold-pressed. The source material is heated or partially cooked to soften the cell walls so that the expeller, which exerts enormous pressure, can extract the oil efficiently from the seed. The oil is subjected to additional heat, created by this enormous pressure. This generated heat is so great that the meal cake, the material remaining after the oil is extracted, is often quite scorched. So, ignore the term 'cold-pressed' when you see it on the label of vegetable oil.

However, it is preferable to obtain *pressed* oil, using an hydraulic or screw press, in which moderate heat has been used, instead of the more common current practice of extracting oils by subjecting them to light petroleum fraction solvents, and then refining and bleaching them. The key word to look for on the label will be 'pressed', 'crude', or 'unrefined'. Avoid oils labelled 'refined' as well as those with added synthetic antioxidants.

If you purchase the unrefined, pressed oils, there will be no need for an artificial preservative to be added, since the crude oil contains natural antioxidants such as carotenoids, vitamin E, and phosphatides. All help to keep the oil fresh.

If you look at the label on a container of refined oil, you see that it usually lists an artificial preservative. The natural antioxidants were destroyed in the refining!

Peanut butter Buy the old-fashioned peanut butter made from 100 per cent peanuts, with no additions other than some salt and unhydrogenated oil.

Peanut flour This is ground peanuts, a rich source of protein.

It can be added to grain flour, but will make the baked product darker and heavier. See note under *barley flour* above.

Peanuts Buy raw peanuts, in the shell, or those that are raw, unsalted, unoiled, and packed in vacuum tins without anti-oxidant.

Pepita seeds See *pumpkin seeds.*

Potato flour This is a natural thickening agent that can be used instead of white flour.

Primary yeast See *brewer's yeast.*

Pumpkin seeds These are rich in nutrients. They are called 'pepita seeds' when they are round rather than flat in shape. See note on *nuts*, above. See also *sunflower seeds*. You can eat peeled pumpkin seeds as they are, or grind them into a meal in a seed grinder or electric blender and add them to cereal or topping for dessert.

Raw sugar In the UK, but not in the rest of Europe, there is a fine assortment of raw sugars which have been subjected to the minimum of refining and processing. The best include Barbados muscavado and Demerara. Avoid pieces, 'brown sugar' and coffee crystals as these are often coloured, refined sugars.

Rice This is a whole grain. Buy brown rice (sometimes called 'health rice').

Rice bran This is a by-product of processing brown rice and consists of the outer bran layers. It is rich in nutrients and can be added to bread dough, biscuits, and cereals.

Rice flour The brown rice when ground produces rice flour –

a heavy flour. It is a flavoursome addition to other flours for baking. See note under *barley flour* above.

Rose hips These are the fruits of the rose. They are gathered, dried and pulverized. They are extremely high in vitamin C and can be used in herb teas. They are also prepared in tablet form. See *acerola,* above.

Rye This is a whole grain that can be cooked or sprouted. For sprouting directions, see pp. 97–98.

Rye flour This is ground from the whole grain, rye.

Rye meal This is a coarsely ground rye flour, suitable for pumpernickel-type bread. It has the consistency of coarse cornmeal.

St-John's-bread See *carob powder.*

Sea salt This is an unrefined salt, containing many minerals. Its source is the sea. This is sometimes sold coarse but may be ground finer with a salt mill or electric coffee grinder or a blender.

Seafoods Buy fresh seafoods that were caught in safe waters and have not been given antibiotic treatment.

Sesame seeds These are rich in nutrients. You can buy them hulled or unhulled. The hull is brown and slightly bitter. The unhulled seeds are white, delicate in flavour, and more perishable. The seeds can be ground in a seed grinder or an electric blender and used on cereal or over dessert. The hulled seeds can be sprouted. See pp. 97–98 for sprouting directions.

Soybeans These dried beans can be used like other dried beans for making baked casseroles, soups, and other dishes.

They are very nourishing, inexpensive, and a boon especially to vegetarians, since they are the only complete protein food from the vegetable kingdom. The dried soybeans can be sprouted. See pp. 97–98 for directions.

Soy flour   The soybean is finely ground, and it is a nourishing addition to other flour for baking. It is not truly a flour in the same sense as grains, but it enriches all baked goods. See note on *barley flour* above. Mixed with water, soy flour can be made into a soy milk. Soy flour is also called 'soy milk powder'. It is available as full-fat soy flour, which is produced from the whole soy bean and is used for general purposes; as minimum-fat soy flour, which is good for making soy milk; and as low-fat soy flour, which is good for baking.

Soy phosphatides   See *Lecithin granules.*

Sunflower-seed meal   This is ground sunflower seeds. It can be sprinkled over cereal or used as a topping for dessert. The meal can be made by grinding hulled sunflower seeds in a seed grinder or an electric blender. Use it promptly to avoid oxidation.

Sunflower seeds   These are rich in nutrients. Buy sunflower seeds that are already hulled. See note on *nuts,* above. See also *pumpkin seeds.*

Sweeteners, natural   See *blackstrap molasses, honey, malt, maple sugar, maple syrup, molasses, raw sugar.* Remember that natural sweeteners are highly concentrated. Use them sparingly.

Syrups   See *blackstrap molasses, honey, malt, maple syrup, molasses.*

Tahini   This paste is made of finely ground sesame seeds. It can be used in salad dressing, as a spread, as a butter substitute, or over vegetables. Mixed with honey, it makes a confection, halvah.

Tapioca   Buy the tapioca that is whole, not pearled. This is a root product from the cassava plant and is made into a well-known pudding.

Tapioca flour   This is a natural thickening agent that can be used instead of white flour.

Thickeners, natural   See *agar-agar, arrowroot starch, gelatin, potato starch, tapioca starch, unbleached flour.*

Triple-rich flour   See *Cornell Mix.*

Unbleached white flour   This is wheat flour from which the bran has been removed. See also *Cornell Mix.* The British practice is usually to vary the extraction rate, that is, the amount of the whole grain allowed to remain in the finished flour. An 81 per cent or 85 per cent extraction is good in recipes requiring unbleached white flour and for most cake making.

Vanilla   Buy pure vanilla extract or the vanilla pod. Do not buy vanillin, a synthetic flavouring.

Vegetable oil   See *oils.*

Vegetable salt   This is a seasoning blended from finely ground and dried vegetables. Sometimes it also contains salt.

Vegetables   Buy fresh ones. In selecting greens, choose the darkest ones you can find. Whenever possible, try to locate organically grown vegetables.

Vinegar   Buy apple-cider vinegar, made from whole, unsprayed apples, or wine vinegar. Do not use white vinegar for food or drink.

Wheat germ This nutritious supplement can be used instead of bread crumbs, added to cereal, baked goods, soups, stews, casseroles, or sprinkled on desserts. Wheat germ is a good source of vitamin E.

Whey This is a nutritious, easily digested milk sugar, available in powder form. It can be added to drinks or baked goods.

Whole wheat berries The grains of whole wheat are called berries. They can be cooked or sprouted. See pp. 97–98 for sprouting directions.

Whole wheat flour The wheat berries should be ground freshly, preferably by stone, to make whole wheat flour. This type of flour is usually labelled '100% Wholemeal'. When possible the flour should be compost grown but quite often a small amount of hard Canadian durum wheat has to be incorporated to improve the bread making qualities. Unbleached flour is rarely compost grown.

Whole wheat (cracked) This is cracked wheat, suitable for cooked cereal.

Wild rice This is a whole grain, although 'rice' is a misnomer. It is a delicious but expensive food.

Yeast See *baking yeast* and *brewer's yeast*.

Yogurt This is a cultured milk beverage. Sometimes it is spelled 'yoghurt' or 'yoghourt'. For its special properties, see note on *buttermilk*, p. 38.

A few items have purposely been omitted from the above list. The following are *not* recommended.

Brown sugar This sweetener is still quite refined. Instead, use the other suggested natural sweeteners.

Cornstarch This natural thickening agent would make a good substitute for white flour, except that in processing, it is apt to be treated with sulphur dioxide.

Cottonseed flour Although flour from the cottonseed is high in protein, it is unacceptable as a food because the cotton crop is subjected to extensive pesticidal spraying. Residues remain in the cottonseed. Instead, use other suggested flours.

Cottonseed oil Although the oil from the cottonseed is a good vegetable oil, it is unacceptable for the same reason as is cottonseed flour, above. Instead, use other suggested vegetable oils.

Soy lecithin spread If this butter substitute has the words 'hydrogenated' or 'partially hydrogenated' or 'hardened' or 'partially hardened' on the label, the product has been subjected to an undesirable processing, and it is best avoided. Instead, use butter and vegetable oils.

Help! Now what?

By now you are probably convinced that you should switch to natural foods. How can you estimate the amounts needed for your own family? The following measures will be helpful. The cup used is an ordinary 8 fluid ounce, straight-sided mug, kept especially for measuring.

One pound of	*will yield in cups*
almonds, shelled	3½
apricots, dried	3½
Brazil nuts, shelled	3
brewer's yeast, flakes	8
butter	2
cashews, shelled	3½
cheese, cottage	2
cheese, natural, hard, grated	4
corn flour (depending on fineness)	3-4
cornmeal	3
coconut, dried, shredded	4
date sugar	2¼
dates, pitted	2
dates, whole	2½
honey	1½
figs, cut up	2⅔
figs, whole	2¾
filberts, shelled	3½
flaxseeds, whole	3
flour, 81% extraction	3¾
maple syrup	2
molasses	1½

One pound of	will yield in cups
oat flour	4½
oil, vegetable	2¼
peaches, dried	3
peanut butter	1¾
peanuts, shelled	3
pecans, shelled	3
prunes, dried	2½
raisins, dried	2½–3
rice polished	2
rye flour	6
sesame seeds, whole	3
soy flour	4
sunflower seeds, whole	4
walnuts, black, shelled	4
walnuts, English, shelled	4
wheat germ	4
wheat flour, unbleached white	4
wheat flour, whole	3½

There are some additional measures that may be useful:

Each ¼-ounce envelope of unflavoured, unsweetened gelatin equals one dessertspoonful.

Each square cake of baking yeast equals one packet of yeast or one dessertspoon of dry yeast granules.

3½ pounds of unshelled almonds yield one pound of shelled nuts; 2¼ pounds of filberts, 1½ pounds of peanuts, 2½ pounds of pecans, 5½ pounds of black walnuts, and 2½ pounds of English walnuts yield one pound each of shelled nuts.

HOW DO YOU HANDLE ORGANIC FOOD?

Once you have managed to buy some organically raised foods, what do you do with them? You have probably exerted effort and spent good money to find them. Naturally, you will want to handle them carefully to conserve their nutritional value.

Some items should be stored immediately in the freezer;

others in the refrigerator; and some will keep well if stored in tight containers in a cool, dry place. It is important to know what goes where. All too often, a bewildered natural food novice will keep many highly perishable items at room temperature in the kitchen, and store those with long shelf life in the freezer!

As you read the following you will realize that a *large* freezer, although not essential, is useful for the natural food enthusiast. If you do not own a freezer but anticipate purchasing one, by all means consider the *largest* one that your budget and room space will allow. A *second* refrigerator, if feasible, is also useful. It will allow you space to store many items that need to be kept cool but not as cold as they would be in your main refrigerator.

If you live in a city flat, with a small kitchen and no freezer except for the ice-cube compartment of the refrigerator, your shopping will have to be limited to small, frequent purchases. The ice-cube compartment is *not* satisfactory for storing frozen foods such as meat, fish, and poultry, since the temperature is not sufficiently low.

Let's pretend that you have arrived home from a shopping trip at a health food store, or that your order has just arrived. How do you store the various foods? What special precautions must you take in handling some of them?

Meat, poultry, fish　Since these foods may be frozen, put them in your home freezer immediately. First check to see that they are well wrapped to prevent freezer burn. If in doubt, apply a second protective wrapping of freezer paper or slip them into clear plastic bags and seal them tightly with wire twisters. It is wise to see that the name of the meat cut or type of fish is clearly written on the wrapper; you can also add the poundage and date. Make certain that your home freezer is set no higher than 0°F (−18° C) for satisfactory storage of these items. Even at 0° F (−18° C) frozen foods have a limited storage life. According to the US Department of Agriculture, the following are the maximum storage periods in months before nutrient losses occur:

beef	6–12
lamb and veal	6–9
pork	3–6
sausage and ground meat	1–3
chickens	6–12
turkeys	3–6

Fish has a storage period similar to beef and chicken. If held too long, fish deteriorates despite low temperatures, because the freezing does not completely inactivate the enzymes nor does it prevent the action of oxygen on the enzymes, which continue to deteriorate at a slow rate. If you have ever thawed out commercially frozen fish that had been stored too long, you have noted the signs of deterioration: excessive drip; tough, dry, darkened or yellowed flesh; and rancid odours and flavours due to decomposition.

Being aware of these facts, plan to use your supply of organ meats and ground meats first, in order not to lose precious nutrients in your protein foods. Then note the techniques of thawing. Most frozen meat may be thawed before cooking or cooked without thawing with equally good results.

The usual cooking methods can be used for thawed meats. If frozen meat is not thawed, extra cooking time is required to allow for thawing. Large frozen roasts may take as much as one and a half times as long to cook as unfrozen roasts of the same size and shape. Small roasts and thin cuts cooked without thawing require varying amounts of cooking time, depending on the size and shape of the cut.

Thawing frozen meat in the refrigerator results in the most uniform thawing and the most attractive appearance, but it takes longer than if the meat is thawed at room temperature. The time for the interior temperature of frozen meat to reach the temperature at which ice crystals start to melt ($28°$ F, $-2°$ C) is two to three times as long in the refrigerator as in the room; two times as long at room temperature as in running water;

and two to three times as long in running water as during cooking.

It is usually best to thaw frozen poultry until it is pliable before cooking. The thawing of poultry in the refrigerator in the original wrapper is recommended by some. To shorten the thawing time, birds sealed in watertight wrapping may be thawed in cold water. After they are thawed they can be cooked in the same ways as fresh poultry. It can be dangerous to undercook frozen poultry.

If you are able to get fresh organic meat and poultry, or fish caught in safe waters, without antibiotic treatment, store them in the refrigerator for short periods only, at a temperature just above freezing. Minced meats and organ meats are highly perishable and should be used promptly.

Meat becomes rancid because of fat oxidation. Meat becomes discoloured because of pigment oxidation. Low temperatures will retard these objectionable changes. Be sure to store meat in the coldest part of the refrigerator.

Tight packaging, which may be convenient and sanitary for handling meats, poultry, and fish at the packing place, encourages the growth of micro-organisms on surfaces. If these flesh foods have been wrapped in transparent film or cardboard trays, remove and rewrap them loosely, allowing for air circulation. Freezer paper is good for this purpose.

If the giblets of the poultry are packed in a separate bag placed inside the whole bird or under the cut-up pieces, remove them. Cover the giblets loosely before refrigerating and use them promptly.

When you are ready to prepare the meat, poultry, or fish, special precautions should be taken. If you feel that the surfaces require cleaning, wipe them with a paper towel that you can discard. Do *not* wash the carcass under a stream of water. By doing this you lose nutrients.

Keep a special cutting board for trimming, cutting, and preparing all raw meat, poultry, and fish. Scour it thoroughly each time you use it, because raw meat, poultry, and fish may contain pathogenic organisms, such as trichinae (responsible for trichinosis), or salmonellae (responsible for salmonellosis). Unfortunately, under the present public health meat and poultry inspection systems these hazardous organisms may not be detected.

The major bacterial contamination occurs on the surface of the raw carcass. For this reason it is imperative that a special cutting board be reserved for raw meat, poultry, and fish. Usually the health of organically raised livestock is better than that of animals from ordinary sources, but don't take chances. Organically raised meat and poultry may be contaminated at inspection time by other carcasses.

Now you understand the importance of using a special cutting board for the preparation of raw vegetables and fruit rather than the one used for cutting raw meat, poultry, and fish. Also, do not underestimate the importance of washing your hands and knives carefully after you have handled these raw foods. Control of bacterial contamination will depend largely on your kitchen habits.

Proper cooking kills disease-carrying bacteria. Searing the outside of meat normally eliminates the hazard. But this is not true with hamburgers, rissoles or other undercooked minced meat products, which may be contaminated throughout. The days of steak tartare are gone completely!

Make it a general rule to request lean meats from your organic source, and trim all visible fat. Meat fat is saturated and is not desirable in large amounts. Even when you have succeeded in trimming all the visible meat fat, remember that you will still be eating fat in meat, since it goes through the tissues in 'marbled' beef. Lamb fat is even more highly saturated than beef fat.

The fat scraps you have cut away need not be wasted. Feed them to the birds in winter. If it is summertime, pack the fat into empty tins or cartons, label, and freeze it for later use. Or you can accumulate the fat scraps in the freezer until you have a sufficient amount to render them and make your own soap.

Fresh produce If you have arrived home from the shopping trip with your organic foods and have properly stored the frozen items, turn next to the fruits and vegetables. Refrigerate them to maintain crispness, and plan to use them promptly. Otherwise there will be a decline of vitamins and enzymes due to long storage.

When you clean leafy salad greens, use a gentle spray of cool water to dislodge any clinging earth or insects. In the absence of pesticides, occasionally insects are found.

Never allow your vegetables to stand soaking in water, a practice that leaches valuable minerals from the foods.

To minimize oxidation, prepare your salads just before eating them. Cut leaves coarsely. The more cut surfaces that are exposed, the greater the degree of oxidation. Add the dressing as soon as you have prepared the salad. The oil, which coats the leaves, helps prevent oxidation. Try to estimate the amount of salad your family will eat, in order to avoid waste. Keep the unused salad greens in a crisper.

Fresh vegetables such as kale, spinach, turnip greens, chard, and broccoli should be refrigerated promptly. They keep their nutrients best near freezing and at high humidity. Cabbage is a fairly stable source of ascorbic acid and has more than most leafy vegetables. Even after two months it will retain three-quarters or more of its ascorbic acid (vitamin C) if it is refrigerated under 40° F (4° C). If you purchase several varieties of vegetables at one time, use the perishable ones first. You can safely count on using the cabbage later.

Some vegetables retain their ascorbic acid well even at room temperature. These include peppers, runner and French beans, lima beans, and tomatoes. Firm, ripe tomatoes can be held at room temperature for several days without losing their ascorbic acid. However, when over-ripe, they lose their value rapidly.

Berries are generally perishable. They can be held for a few days in the refrigerator. Keep them cold, dry, and whole to retain their nutrients. Do not cap, stem, or bruise berries until you plan to use them.

Citrus fruits retain their high content of ascorbic acid even when they are not refrigerated. There is a loss of nutritive value if oranges are squeezed and the juice is strained.

Carrots, sweet potatoes, potatoes, and other roots and tubers retain their most important nutrients reasonably well outside of the refrigerator, provided they are kept cool and moist enough to prevent withering. However, they spoil quickly if they are in direct contact with water formed from condensation. Keep potatoes out of the light, and discard any green skin, or sprouts, both of which are toxic.

Freshly dug potatoes are highest in ascorbic acid, although potatoes are not an outstanding source of this vitamin. Immature potatoes have more ascorbic acid than those left to mature. The loss is progressive throughout the storage period, so that after three months of storage only about half is left. After six months potatoes retain only about a third of their original content of ascorbic acid. Hence keep storage periods brief.

Keep bananas, avocados, pears, and mangoes at room temperature. To hasten their ripening, place them in closed paper bags. Use bananas only after all the green has disappeared from the skin. They are ripe when they are completely yellow and begin to develop brown flecks. If you are not certain whether an avocado is ripe, cut out a thin wedge. If the flesh is still hard, carefully replace the wedge and wrap the avocado in a plastic bag, excluding air. Check daily.

Melons should be ripened at room temperature. Check daily.

Eggs If you are fortunate enough to locate a farm where roosters are present among free-ranging hens, the eggs produced will probably be fertile. Refrigerate such eggs promptly. They are more perishable than non-fertile ones and have a shorter shelf life.

All eggs should be refrigerated promptly, since their flavour deteriorates more quickly at room temperature. Long storage produces other changes: the thick white gets thin; the yolk membrane weakens and may break when the shell is opened. All eggs should be used promptly.

Eggshells are porous and allow for passage of moisture, bacteria, and moulds. Hence it is better to store the eggs in a covered container than to use the open egg slots provided in the doors of some refrigerators. The *papier-mâché* cartons in which eggs have traditionally been sold serve as good refrigerator containers.

Do not wash eggs before putting them in the refrigerator. If you wish to wash them, do so just before you use them.

For many years health-conscious people have been wary of using raw egg white in quantity or regularly. This caution was based on a much-publicized fact that avidin, a substance found in raw egg white, combines with biotin, one of the B vitamins, and prevents it from reaching the blood. In the last decade another problem has developed that makes it unwise to eat raw eggs, yolks as well as whites. Salmonellae, the pathogenic organisms mentioned earlier (see p. 58) are a frequent contaminant of eggs. For this reason it is imperative not to use cracked eggs. They are more apt to be contaminated than sound ones, although *all* raw eggs are suspect. It is wiser to use cooked eggs rather than raw ones. Cooking kills the salmonellae. Organically produced eggs should be raised in clean surroundings and come from healthy hens. The salmonellosis problem is probably less prevalent on such farms than on ordinary ones. However contamination is so widespread that caution is necessary.

Fresh dairy products Milk, cream, butter, and cheeses are perishable and should be refrigerated promptly. The storage temperature of 40° F or 4° C, is desirable to protect the flavour and food values of dairy products. They should be tightly wrapped so that they do not absorb odours or flavours of other stored foods.

Exposure to light harms the flavour and decreases the riboflavin (part of the vitamin B complex) in milk. If you purchase certified raw milk, and it is sold in a clear glass bottle, transfer it to a sterilized dark-coloured bottle or other light-excluding container. Or, if you prefer, remove the light bulb from your refrigerator and cover the exposed socket. Or merely loosen the bulb so that it does not light up when the door is opened. The soft cheeses, such as cottage cheese, are highly perishable. They should be stored, tightly covered, in the coldest part of the refrigerator at temperatures just above freezing.

The hard natural aged cheeses, such as Cheddar, Edam, Gouda, Emmenthaler, or Gruyère, should be wrapped tightly before they are refrigerated to protect them from exposure to air. The original wrapping is usually satisfactory if it fits tightly and excludes air. Once you have cut into the cheese, there are several ways to handle it in order to extend its shelf life. You can purchase a special container for cheese storage, which usually has a section at the bottom in which you place a mixture of vinegar and water, a divided perforated section in which the cheese is placed, and a tightly fitting cover.

Or, more simply, you can reserve a clean towel for wrapping around the cheese. Soak the towel in a mixture of water and apple-cider vinegar, wring out the cloth so that it is moist but not dripping, and wrap it around the cheese, which has already been wrapped in heavy parchment paper or freezer paper. When the towel begins to dry out, moisten it again in a water-apple-cider-vinegar mixture. Another method of preventing hard cheese from drying out after it is cut is to try to keep the original wrapping intact and seal all cut surfaces of the cheese with a thin layer of butter or vegetable oil. The exposed cheese surface will not dry out or mould.

Hard cheeses will keep well at refrigerator temperatures. Just before using the cheese, trim off any surface mould that forms. Save it to feed the birds or, if you wish, to bait mouse traps. Your choice will reflect your personal philosophy!

To protect the flavour of butter, store it, tightly wrapped and covered, in the coldest part of the refrigerator, preferably at 40° F (4° C), or lower. Exclusion of air will protect the fat from reacting with oxygen to produce a rancid flavour and odour. If you detect any rancidity, discard the butter. Rancid fats and oils have toxic properties and are threats to the heart, liver, and integrity of the body oils from which the glands manufacture hormones, and are reported to be a predisposing factor to cancer.

If you are able to get raw butter, made from certified raw cream, remember that it is even more perishable than pasteurized butter. The same is true for fresh butter, which is more perishable than salted butter, since the salt acts as a preservative. For this reason, purchase butter in limited amounts, wrap it tightly in freezer paper, freeze it, and thaw out small portions of it at a time.

If your refrigerator has a butter compartment, use it for storing small items such as supplements, but do not use it for butter storage. Both warmth and light hasten the development of rancidity.

Breads and baked goods   Breads and simple yeast cakes, made without custards, store well in the freezer. Many can be frozen in their original wrappers. If you are in doubt, apply a second protective wrapper of freezer paper, or use a clear plastic bag, and seal tightly with a wire twister.

Bread can be thawed out quickly if you are surprised by unexpected company and are caught short in your supply. Just drop the pre-sliced frozen bread into a bread toaster. Otherwise thaw bread at room temperature for several hours.

To restore frozen baked goods to freshness, thaw, and heat gently in a 200° F, 93° C, oven just before serving.

If you buy whole grain breads or baked goods and intend using them in a fresh state, refrigerate them. Do not store them at room temperature or in a bread box. Remember that these products will be free of preservatives or mould retarders. Thus the shelf life is shorter than for ordinary commercial baked goods. Their shelf life can be extended, however, through refrigeration. This is especially true in humid summer weather.

Whole grain flours and cereals Whole wheat berries or grains of rye, oats, corn, buckwheat, and millet have a long storage life when left intact in nature's own packaging, provided they are kept cool and dry in tightly closed containers. However, oxidation takes place rapidly once the grain is milled finely into flour or coarsely into cereal. Rancidity is not usually detected by either smell or taste. For this reason it is wise to purchase flour and cereal in small amounts and use them promptly. They should be refrigerated, or if space permits, put into the freezer. If you find it better to purchase large quantities of flour and cereal, repackage these items in small plastic bags when they arrive. Exclude as much air as possible and seal them tightly with wire twisters. Make certain to mark them with the date and type of flour or cereal, then freeze them. Transfer single bags to the refrigerator as you plan to use them.

Vegetable oils If you can't locate crude, pressed vegetable oils in dark bottles or tins, store oils that have been bottled in clear glass, unopened, in a cool, dark cupboard. As soon as you open a bottle, decant into a dark bottle or tin of approximately the same size. Cap the bottle or tin tightly after each use to exclude the air, and keep the oil refrigerated. The one exception is olive oil, which seems to keep best at an even room temperature.

Dried fruits Organically raised dried fruits have not been processed with sulphur dioxide, nor have they been treated with fumigants. For this reason they will keep best stored in the refrigerator, especially during hot, humid weather, when they are apt to mould.

The natural sugars in these fruits give them a long shelf life, provided they are kept cool. At times these natural sugars may exude to the surface of the fruit and appear as small, granular deposits. This does *not* indicate spoilage. The fruit is still edible.

Nuts and Seeds As with grains, nuts and seeds have a long storage life in nature's own packaging when left intact, provided they are kept cool and dry in tightly closed containers. If you buy nuts in the shell, you can crack them as you use them. However, if you consider this an onerous job – as most people do – purchase bagged or vacuum-packed shelled, raw, unsalted nuts. To preserve their freshness once the container is open, store the remainder in the refrigerator. Or, if space permits, put them in clear plastic bags in the freezer. Exclude as much air as possible from the opened container, since nuts oxidize and become rancid.

Sunflower and pumpkin seeds are generally sold already hulled and are available in bags or are vacuum-packed. They should be handled like the nuts.

Sesame seeds are sold unhulled or hulled. The unhulled seeds have a long shelf life, provided they are stored in a tightly closed container and kept cool and dry. The hulled seeds should be refrigerated and used promptly, since their shelf life is far shorter.

Natural sweeteners Honey and unsulphured molasses, unlike most natural foods, have a long shelf life. Because of their concentrated sweetness, both can be kept for long periods of time at room temperature without spoilage, even after the jars have been opened. If honey is refrigerated or placed in a cold room, it may crystallize. This is a natural condition and does *not* indicate spoilage. Honey can be used in the crystallized state – indeed, some people prefer it – or it can be made liquid again. Simply place the jar of honey in a pan of warm but not hot water to dissolve the crystals. Be certain to use mild heat, not exceeding 129° F (54° C), in order not to spoil the flavour or destroy the nutrients.

Once the container is opened, maple syrup will eventually mould. For this reason, once the seal is broken, keep the syrup refrigerated and use it within a reasonable time. If mould develops, carefully skim it off the top. This does not injure the flavour of the rest of the maple syrup.

If you open a large container of maple syrup and do not intend using all of it at once, you can pasteurize the remainder in small individual containers, using sterilized preserving jars, rubber rings, and caps.

Store raw sugar in a humid place. If it dries out and goes hard, cover with a moist cloth and in a day it will be back to normal.

A few miscellaneous items Powdered kelp will not cake. Neither will the large, rough crystals of earth or sea salt. All of these items should be stored in tightly closed jars in a cool, dry place. None needs refrigeration.

Both lecithin granules and lecithin liquid can be stored at room temperature. Seasonal conditions may create some variations in the colour, taste, and appearance of the granules, but these changes do not affect their quality. The jar or tin of liquid lecithin should be kept tightly closed to exclude air.

Baking-yeast granules should be stored in a cool, dry place in a tightly covered container. The granules are active for at least six months and require no refrigeration.

Brewer's yeast, flake or powder, also requires no refrigeration and can be stored in a cool, dry place in a tightly covered container.

Once a package of non-fat dry milk powder is opened, even a small percentage of moisture can double or triple the bacteria count. For this reason store the powder in a tightly closed container, keep it cool, and use it within a reasonable time.

Old-fashioned peanut butter should be refrigerated once the jar has been opened. If the oil separates from the spread, make certain that the jar is tightly closed, and store it inverted. When you uncap it, stir the oil back into the spread.

Carob powder, whole flaxseed, agar-agar, gelatin, Irish moss, soybeans, lentils, whole dried beans, rose hips, and vinegar do not have any special storage requirements. They can be kept in their original containers, and should be stored in a cool dry place.

How do you prepare natural foods?

Gradually you've eliminated all the junk foods from your kitchen. You've invested in highly nutritious and potentially delicious basic foodstuffs. What's the next step? Meal planning.

You will need to learn a few precepts and practise them repeatedly until they become habitual. Once you perform them quite automatically, you may wonder why, at first, they seemed to be so overwhelming.

For years nutritionists have been talking about the 'basic four' foods as a daily guide to fitness. Keep this in mind as you shop and plan your meals. Use the 'basic four' as a checklist. The list is sound fundamentally, but I recommend a few modifications.

'Basic Four' Groups	*Modifications*
Protein Foods	
2 or more servings daily: Beef, veal, pork, lamb, poultry, fish, and eggs	3 servings daily: Same list, but omit veal and pork unless organically raised.
Alternatives: Dry beans, dry peas, nuts	Alternatives: Same list, but serve a complete protein with the dry beans, dry peas or nuts. Add soybeans to the list.
Produce Foods	
4 or more servings daily: Include a citrus fruit or any other fruit or vegetable that is a good source for vitamin C; a dark-	4 or more servings daily: Same list, with the recommendation that fruits be eaten raw and that at least half of the vegetables

green or deep-yellow vegetable that is a good source for vitamin A – at least every other day; other vegetables and fruits, including potatoes

be eaten raw, in salad. Add sprouts to the list.

Dairy Foods

Some milk for everyone daily:
children – 3 to 4 cups
teenagers – 4 or more cups
adults – 2 or more cups

Milk preferably in form of yogurt, kefir, tette, kumiss, clabber, buttermilk, or other lactic-acid ferment; natural cheeses, cottage cheese. This list includes, for the sake of travellers, a number of nutritious national milk specialities.

Grain Foods

4 or more servings daily:
Whole grain, enriched or restored
Plus other foods as needed to complete meals and to provide additional food energy and other food values

1 or 2 servings daily:
Whole grain or triple-enriched Cornell formula
Plus unrefined vegetable oil or butter; honey, or other natural sweetener in limited amount; and nutritional supplements

The modifications deserve some explanation. Veal may be an unacceptable food because of present-day methods of animal rearing. Milk-fed veal is apt to be an anaemic animal, reared on a restricted diet to keep the flesh light-coloured. Pork is unacceptable for several reasons. Present-day methods of rearing are apt to be poor. The animal's fat content is high. Smoked meats, such as bacon or ham, should be avoided because smoked meats are suspected of having cancer-inciting properties. Heavy use of salt is undesirable – and these meats are loaded with it. The use of sodium nitrate and/or sodium nitrite as a colour fixative and preservative is undesirable.

If you wish to eat veal, obtain it from an organic source. If you wish to eat pork, limit your intake to unsmoked varieties, such as pork chops or pork roast, from organic sources, and trim off all visible fat. Eat fish, fowl, lean beef and lamb, or eggs daily, and depend on them for complete protein foods at each meal.

Dry beans and peas, as well as nuts, are incomplete proteins. That is, they all lack some of the essential amino acids. In order for the meal to be well balanced, legumes should be combined with proteins that are complete, such as the ones mentioned above. The one exception is soybean, which *is* a complete protein from the vegetable kingdom.

It is advisable to eat as much fruit and as many vegetables as possible in a raw state in order to preserve nutrients, including ascorbic acid and precious enzymes. The addition of sprouts (see pp. 97–98) to the daily menu is desirable.

Dairy foods, if tolerated, are preferable in a lactic-acid fermented form. If obtainable, certified raw milk, cream, and raw butter, made from certified raw cream, are desirable. While the dairy foods offer valuable contributions of calcium and other nutrients, they should not be considered in the same primary class as proteins and produce. Indeed, man is the only animal that uses dairy products beyond the weaning stage, and Americans are probably larger consumers of dairy products than people elsewhere. Those who subscribe to a belief that milk and dairy products – even those of good quality – should not be consumed by adults, may find some reassurance in the fact that the Eskimos, the Maori, the Australian aborigines, as well as other groups of people whose traditional diets did *not* include dairy products, nevertheless maintained themselves in good health.

By the same token, grain foods should not be considered in the same primary class as protein and produce. Although we can recognize their useful role – especially in times of emergencies, such as famine or war – they do not offer the same high biological quality of the protein and produce groups. In addition, many grains are poorly tolerated and are frequently allergens. If you tolerate grains, by all means use the whole grains rather than those that are degerminated. If you cannot tolerate whole grains, try the Cornell formula (see pp. 101). Wheat bran may be rich in nutrients, but its proteins are digested with great difficulty and are only partially utilized.

The roughage of bran makes it intolerable for many people, a fact that has long been recognized. In addition, wheat bran has been a major food source of strontium 90 contamination since nuclear testing began.

As with dairy foods, grains have not always played a role in good diets. Eskimos and other primitive peoples have enjoyed robust health without grains in their traditional diets. Through the aggressive efforts of millers and bakers, abetted by governmental policy, grains and grain products continue to be highly overrated.

Other foods needed for complete meals to provide additional energy and other values include unrefined vegetable oil and a limited quantity of butter. Although the orthodox nutritionist allows items such as sugary foods and beverages, we will shun them. By the time you have filled your daily quota of necessities from the 'basic four' groups, you will find little or no room left for junk!

There is, however, a place for nutritional supplements. This may surprise you, and I can hear you asking, 'But if you eat so well, why should you have to use supplements?'

There are several sound reasons. Even when you make wise food selections, there is a good chance that by the time the food reaches your plate it has lost nutrients. To begin with, many foods are not grown on mineralized, fertile soil. Many are not picked at their peak of goodness. Most have travelled long distances and have been in stores for a while. Even after you bring them home, there may be additional storage time. Then you wash and cut them, and they may be cooked. Each step along the way has tended to reduce nutrients, particularly enzymes and trace elements. The latter may vary from place to place, soil to soil, and may not be in balanced amounts in individual foods.

Additionally, many of us suffer from deficiencies due to past poor eating habits. Supplements offer a possibility to make up for these past errors. If depletion is not too severe, the effects may be checked or even reversed.

Furthermore, most of us live in stressful situations, either from outside work pressures or emotional strains within ourselves. Supplements can help us meet these daily challenges better.

We are living in a polluted environment. Car exhaust, cigarette smoke, incinerator fumes, industrial wastes, and other noxious materials constantly assault us and add to what has been termed 'the total body burden'. Supplements can play a vital role as buffering and detoxifying agents, since chemical and toxic agents deplete the body both of enzymes and vitamins.

However, the supplements should contain enzymes and trace elements in addition to well-balanced minerals and vitamins. If any essentials are lacking, the supplements may not only be worthless but can contribute to further imbalances in the body chemistry.

Some people take daily supplements as preventatives, viewing them as insurance for future health. Since many natural supplements are merely concentrated foods, they can be worked into meal preparations. These include wheat germ, brewer's yeast, desiccated liver, kelp, dulse, and rose hips.

Familiarize yourself with the 'basic four' groups as modified. (See p. 68). Note that the two major groups are proteins and produce foods. Work each meal around these two groups, since they are the 'protective foods'. Fill in with the dairy and grain groups, which are secondary. With this in mind, try planning the meals for a day. These might be typical selections.

Breakfast:
  Fresh fruits, berries, or melons in season, with yogurt
  Egg/s, plus whole grain bread and butter
  Hot beverage (optional)

Lunch:
  Raw vegetable salad, with oil in dressing, plus sprouted
    seed shoots

Roast beef
Brown rice
Buttermilk, plus additional beverage (optional)
Apple

Supper:
Cole slaw salad, with oil in dressing
Baked fish
Steamed broccoli
Jacket potato
Orange
Beverage (optional)

If you check the daily food guide of the 'basic four', you will note that the day's menu above meets all requirements. There is ample choice within the groups to allow for varied meals from day to day. Choices you make within the groups will allow you to select favourite foods for your family, as well as those that are in season and fit into your budget. There is no single way to eat for health. Many different combinations of foods can give the essentials needed for an adequate diet. But choose as great a variety as possible, and practise daily until planning your menu around the modified listing of the 'basic four' becomes automatic.

HOW CAN YOU ORGANIZE YOUR MEAL PREPARATION?

I'll give you a step-by-step description of how I organize my own meal preparation. I don't consider my method the *only* or even the *best* one. But since it works easily and quickly for me, perhaps it will be helpful for you too. Let's follow the supper menu suggested above. Assume that I am preparing the meal for a family of six.

First I set the table. This may amuse you, but setting the table seems to put me in the right mood for working with food. I enjoy using different sets of dishes and serving plates as background for the foods being served. Colour combinations are important to make foods look appetizing. Also, it makes good sense to handle dishes, cutlery, and glassware while my hands are still dry and untouched by food.

I survey the table and check to see that everything is arranged This minimizes last-minute crises, with the cook jumping up and rushing for the forgotten salad bowls or napkins. When I sit down to eat I like to remain seated. It is good for my digestion and more pleasant for my table companions. No one enjoys eating with a frenzied cook. There should be a place for graciousness in living and in dining.

Since both the broccoli and jacket potatoes – the two vegetables chosen for this particular supper – are quite colourful, I shall use white serving bowls. Fish being quite pale, I choose a bright-green platter. The serving dishes will also be bright green. The cole slaw will be served in the usual large wooden salad bowl. Since cabbage is pale, I make a quick mental note to add a few colourful garnishes, which also give interesting flavours and nutrients. I choose small white plates for the oranges.

After the table is set, and while my hands are still dry, I scurry around the kitchen, grouping together the various utensils I shall need for the meal preparation. I place the items on working surfaces, as follows:

Orange preparation Cutting board, potato peeler, paring knife, plastic bag

Jacket potatoes Vegetable scrubbing brush, steamer, stainless steel saucepan and cover

Broccoli Pyrex baking dish, cutting board, sharp knife

Cole slaw Shredder, large bowl

Dishes Large serving tray, on which I place six dessert

dishes, six spoons, two vegetable bowls, fish platter, serving implements

After assembling these items I gather all the others I shall need from the pantry and refrigerator for the meal preparation. I use large trays. By gathering them all at one time, I save steps and minimize the opening and closing of the refrigerator. Do I sometimes forget items? Of course I do! However, I enjoy playing a game with myself, trying to see how efficiently I remember everything.

Using trays, I carry to the kitchen six oranges, a jar of shredded dried coconut, ten potatoes, a bunch of broccoli, three pounds of fresh fish, a tin of vegetable oil, a jar of dried wholemeal breadcrumbs, sprigs of fresh parsley, a head of cabbage, a jar of homemade salad dressing, a jar of sprouts, a tomato, and a carrot. I unload various items at different work surfaces, near the utensils and implements that will be used with them.

By this time it may have occurred to you that my planning has been working backward from the order of the menu. This is correct. Invariably I begin with the dessert.

I wash the oranges and peel the skins with a potato peeler, being careful to leave the layer of white membrane intact. This white membrane contains vitamin P, a valuable fraction of the vitamin C complex. After peeling all the oranges I place them in a plastic bag and refrigerate them. Yes, this is an extra trip to the refrigerator!

Still working backward from the menu, I scrub the skins of the potatoes with a vegetable brush, place them on the oven rack, and set the oven heat at 350° F (177° C). I note the time.

Then I turn my attention to the broccoli. It is rinsed briefly under a gentle stream of cold water. I cut away the tough sections of the stems, break the flowerettes into manageable pieces, and arrange them in a stainless-steel steamer (see p. 81). I lower the steamer into a stainless-steel saucepan with ½ cup of water in the bottom. I cover the saucepan with a tight-fitting lid, set the pot on the stove, but do *not* turn on the heat. Not yet.

Next I place the raw fish on the special cutting board (see p. 58) and cut the fish fillets into individual portions. (This is easier with raw fish than with cooked fish.) I arrange the pieces in the baking pan and pour a little vegetable oil over them. Then I turn the pieces over and pour additional oil on the surfaces. This prevents the fish from sticking to the pan or drying out. Over the top of each piece I sprinkle wholemeal breadcrumbs, mixed dried herbs, and sweet paprika. I place the baking dish on an empty surface in the kitchen, glance swiftly at the clock for a time check, and continue with the last operation of the meal – the salad.

Since salad should be served crisp and fresh, it makes sense to prepare it last, as close to serving time as possible. I wash and trim the cabbage, carrot, parsley, and tomato. Using my shredder (see p. 81), I cut both the cabbage and carrot and let the shreds drop into a large bowl. I add seed sprouts – today's being fenugreek – and immediately cover the salad with dressing. After tossing it well I transfer the salad to the large wooden salad bowl. Then I slice the tomato, mince the parsley, and use both as garnishes on top. I have remembered to reserve some of the parsley as a fish garnish.

In our household we are accustomed to eat our salad as a first course. It starts the digestive juices flowing and prepares the stomach for the foods that follow. The body seems to accept cooked foods better when they are preceded by raw ones.

At this point we are ready to eat! Quickly I gather up all the orange rinds and broccoli stems from the sink and put them into a container reserved for scraps that go into the compost pit.

I test the potatoes with a fork to make certain that they will be ready to serve in another ten minutes. They are fine. Before closing the oven door I pop the fish dish into the oven. I place the pot of broccoli on a medium heat.

The salad is on the table. We are ready to sit down. The fish, broccoli, and jacket potatoes will be ready to serve by the time we have finished our salad.

I assemble my family. Even the best of food will not be beneficial unless it is eaten in a pleasant atmosphere. We try to make certain that this added ingredient is present at meal-times.

After we finish our salad I clear the bowls from the table, and the main course is ready. Fish protein cooks quickly. Long cooking merely dries it out. The broccoli still retains its vivid colour and is slightly on the crisp side – a far cry from the soggy restaurant vegetable languishing on a steam table all day. The jacket potatoes are ready.

After the main part of the dinner is over, dishes are collected, scraped, and stacked. While others are chatting I put the finishing touches on the dessert. The chilled oranges are sliced, arranged on the dessert dishes, and topped with dried coconut shreds, as an 'orange ambrosia'.

The aftermath? Hopefully there is no leftover salad. The mineral-rich water from the steamed broccoli is carefully saved as precious soup stock or for steaming another vegetable for the next day. I am in utter despair when I see an unenlightened housewife pouring such liquids down the sink drain. Any remaining broccoli may be ground in an electric blender and added to the vegetable soup, or may be served cold at another meal – thus avoiding reheating – in a *mélange* of cooked diced carrots, potatoes, corn, and other vegetable bits, topped with homemade dressing. Any leftover potatoes may be blended with muffin or bread dough.

Was this supper simple to prepare? Of course. Did it take much preparation time? No. Some novices seem to think that natural foods take longer to prepare than regular ones. While it may be true that I spend time washing, trimming, and cutting vegetables and fruits, I do not spend time in preparing fancy sauces, mashing potatoes, rolling piecrusts, or fixing fancy desserts. The actual preparation time for cooking brown rice or baking a potato is nominal. Fruit desserts are not time-consuming. There are fewer pots and pans to be washed. Judging from my own experience, I think that I actually spend *less* time in meal preparations now than formerly.

Of course the step-by-step description I have given you for one meal does not apply to all menus. For example, if the protein for the meal consisted of meat or poultry, I would probably have reversed some of the procedure, since these foods take longer to cook than fish. Or if I were serving apples or grapes for dessert, there would have been less work involved than peeling the oranges. I might have washed and arranged these fruits on dessert dishes any time during the work schedule when it suited my convenience.

If your family prefers to eat salad as an accompaniment to the main dish, or if you prefer to have everything on the table at the same time, you can still follow the procedure I have described without modifying it drastically. You would put the fish into the oven and begin to cook the broccoli at the point that you begin to prepare the salad.

What equipment do you need?

Be practical, and use what you have. Just as you will start on natural foods with wise selections in the supermarket, and gradually discard certain items, use a similar approach in your kitchen. Don't rush out and buy special equipment. Go slowly, and decide what you really need. You may wish to make your purchases gradually so that the budget is not strained. Decide whether an item is merely a gadget that will be rarely used, or if it is a basic piece of equipment to be used daily.

Some of the items I have found to be basic are not necessarily expensive. Some are very cheap items from chain stores. Others are more costly. All are sturdily constructed and safe to use.

If I were to draw up a list of necessities for the novice, perhaps a bride-to-be who has not yet bought any kitchen equipment, what items would I include? My list would include things that I have found most useful for daily food preparation. You may be surprised to learn that my list includes only two electric appliances: a blender and a seed grinder. As for other electrical kitchen appliances, I consider many as non-essential and others as anti-environmental. (Faced with the threat of the proliferation of nuclear power plants because of increased electricity demands, I prefer to minimize my power consumption.)

My list is surprisingly short. It consists of a shredder, one or two steamers, a kitchen timer clock, a wall magnet to hold knives, at least one good paring knife, a bread knife, a potato peeler, and a rubber spatula.

The reasons for my choices? I find that an electric blender is indispensable for the type of food preparation that I do. I keep it on the kitchen counter near an electric outlet, ready for work at all times. I prefer the type in which the glass container can be disassembled for cleaning. Thus I am able to prepare salad dressings, mince parsley, chop onions, blend pâtés, and make purées. An electric blender has additional value for mothers with young children, families with elderly people, or invalids on special diets.

A rubber spatula is helpful to push down the food in the container of the electric blender, as well as for removing it. Some of these spatulas are sold with half-inch-wide blades, intended for scraping out the contents of baby-food jars. Such spatulas are ideal for the blender. If you find only one-inch-wide blades, you can trim them down with a pair of scissors. Be certain to round off the edges smoothly.

If you don't wish to invest in an electric blender immediately, is there an alternative? Yes, provided you are willing to use several different pieces of equipment that you may already own. If you have a meat mincer, an egg beater, and a grater, put them to use. However, even when these tools are used, they will not substitute for all of the operations that the blender will perform.

An electric seed grinder is helpful for grinding small seeds, such as sesame and flaxseed, as well as small amounts of raw nuts or fresh coconut. It is also useful for grinding flavouring seeds, such as cardamom, celery, dill, fennel, or caraway. It is advisable to clean the grinder after each operation so that the oil from the seeds or nuts does not remain in the bowl. An easy way to do this is to cut a piece of facial tissue in strips, place them in the seed grinder, put the cover on securely, and press the switch for a few seconds. The paper will be shredded finely and will dislodge the food remnants. Discard the paper, and you will note that the grinder is clean. Each time you use the grinder remember to unplug it *before* you remove the cover. Since these grinders have press buttons rather than switches, you might inadvertently press against the button, with dire consequences. To prolong the life of a seed grinder, grind for brief periods only. If you find that nuts such as filberts get caught under the blade in the bowl, fill the bowl with sesame seeds first, and place the filberts on top. Or, while grinding the filberts, tip the grinder slightly in your hands. Be certain that the cover is secure.

If you don't wish to invest in an electric seed grinder immediately, is there an alternative? Yes, an old-fashioned mortar and pestle will work. So will a suribachi, available in stores selling Japanese items. Or, if you have an electric blender, you can grind seeds and nuts. However, the seed grinder works more efficiently.

A shredder seemed like a big investment to me when I first purchased mine, more than ten years ago. It has been in constant use, continues to function well, and still looks spanking new. In a few minutes I can grate an entire head of cabbage, shred a bunch of raw beets, dice a bunch of carrots, or slice a large turnip. I use it daily for salads as well as in the preparation of vegetables for steaming.

If you don't wish to invest in a shredder immediately, is there an alternative? Yes, buy a set of flat metal graters, with various hole sizes. Be careful not to skin your knuckles.

A stainless-steel collapsible steamer is excellent for cooking vegetables while retaining their bright colour, crispness, flavour, and nutrients. You merely place the diced, sliced, or whole vegetable (such as green peas) in the steamer, lower it into a saucepan containing some liquid at the bottom, cover it tightly, and cook briefly. You will learn how versatile the steamer is after you begin to use it. For example, you can place a clove of garlic in the steaming water without actually placing it in the vegetables. The steamer is good for reheating leftover rice or porridge without drying them out. You can also use the steamer as a colander or sprouting container.

Although aluminium steamers are available, invest in sturdy, safe stainless-steel models. They will fit any size pot. They fold up, like a closing flower, for easy storage. If you can buy two steamers, so much the better. There may be occasions when you wish to serve two steamed vegetables at the same meal.

If you don't wish to invest in a stainless-steel steamer or two immediately, is there an alternative? Yes, you can improvise by making use of a collapsed salad-draining basket or a round cake-cooling rack, provided that they are not made of aluminium.

A kitchen timer clock is indispensable. Some are already built-in features in cooking stoves. The timer is essential if you steam vegetables briefly, depend on exact timing for a pressure cooker, or are making biscuits or a roast. I like the portable type. I can pocket it in my apron as I prepare to go outdoors for fifteen minutes to pull weeds before the bread is ready to be taken out of the oven, or to join some guests in the living room before the soufflé is ready.

If you don't wish to invest in a kitchen timer clock immediately, is there an alternative? Yes, simply borrow the alarm clock from your bedroom!

A wall magnet bar, which holds knives, makes it possible to place these important tools near a working surface. You will be able to see at a glance which knife you need for a particular cutting or trimming operation. In addition, the wall bar offers a safety feature. You will not get your hands nicked or slashed by sharp-bladed tools in kitchen drawers. Since the hollow-ground blades do not cling to the magnet as well as other types of blades, I have treated myself to *two* wall magnets. They are mounted horizontally, parallel to each other, and separated by a six-inch space. The tips of the knife blades touch the top bar, and the sections of the knife blades near the handles touch the bottom bar. The hollow-ground blades no longer slip.

If you don't wish to buy a wall magnet bar, is there an alternative? Yes, have a handy person construct a simple wooden frame to hang on the wall, with slots in the top, into which you can slip the hanging knives, handles up and blades down.

Since you will be preparing lots of fresh vegetables and fruits, it is essential to have good paring and cutting knives. Find at least one that you enjoy using and guard it from those kitchen intruders who would use it to pry off jar caps or as a substitute screwdriver.

Good homemade bread can be mutilated if you lack a satisfactory bread knife. If you plan to bake bread, invest in a knife that will do justice to your handiwork. At one point I had decided to buy a new bread knife. I announced to my family that I would not purchase one until I had tried it. The others were curious to know how I intended carrying out such a plan. It was simple. On our next shopping excursion I carried a loaf of my bread and a bread board. The cutlery saleswoman commented favourably on my practical idea. I succeeded in finding a knife that satisfied me, bought it, and have used it ever since. Yes, the cutlery saleswoman was left smiling and holding a sample of my bread.

The potato peeler, used mainly for peeling oranges (see p. 75), is another inexpensive item. I have learned to travel with one, and I carried it in my pocket all through the Mediterranean area, enjoying the oranges available everywhere. It accompanies me on every picnic or car excursion. In addition to peeling oranges with it, I remove cheese rinds as well as the wax-coated skins of supermarket cucumbers and turnips. I rarely use it for peeling potatoes, since we eat ours baked in the jackets.

HOW ABOUT POTS AND PANS?

Today the housewife is faced with a far greater variety of materials than formerly. For the bride-to-be making initial purchases, pots should be chosen that are scratch-resistant, durable, not liable to the chemical action of foods, and easy to clean. Choices should be limited to basic individual pieces

6

that will be used frequently, rather than expensive sets including some utensils rarely used.

What pots and pans are available, and what are their special features? The following list will describe the main features and drawbacks.

Aluminium This is widely used since it conducts heat rapidly and evenly. The thicker the ware, the better the heat is held and distributed. However, when aluminium is used to cook or store acid fruits or rhubarb, or foods or beverages containing acids or vinegar, minute quantities of the aluminium are dissolved. This is demonstrable, even if water is boiled in an aluminium vessel. Aluminium pots become discoloured when they are in contact with alkaline foods, hard water, or detergents. They become pitted from salty water or salty food. Pitting occurs also when the water contains even minute traces of copper, as it does when it flows through copper piping, now very common in homes. The presence of other metals in the water supply can also present a similar problem. Minute traces of arsenic and fluorides – impurities frequently present in cooking-utensil-grade aluminium – may compound the problem. These metals may also be released into the food when the aluminium dissolves. Increasingly it is becoming evident that repeated exposure to minute quantities of substances over long periods of time can exert profound influences. There have been medical journal reports of a wide range of health problems traced to the use of aluminium vessels for cooking or storing food. For these reasons the choice of aluminium pots and pans is open to question.

Cast iron Iron pots, long in use, hold the heat well. They are heavy to handle. Each time they are used they should be coated with unsalted fat to prevent rusting. Some nutritionists have expressed the belief that one of the reasons that so many people presently show iron-deficiency signs is that old-fashioned cast-iron pots are no longer used. Some of the iron from the pots combines with food – even though it is in a form that is not easily assimilated.

Clay earthenware casseroles These attractive pots are good for long, low-heat oven cooking. They can be used as serving bowls at the table. However, *improper* glazes can release lead and result in poisoning.

Copper These utensils are attractive and are usually lined with another metal. But because of the possibility of poisoning from copper dissolved from pots and pans used for food and drink, they are undesirable for cooking. They are best reserved only for decorative use, unless properly tinned and in first-class condition.

Enamelled or porcelained ware The modern ones are more durable and more resistant to cracking and chipping than those of earlier vintage. It is claimed that the exterior finishes do not interfere with the transfer of heat to the food inside the utensils. Such pots should be discarded if they become cracked or chipped on the inside.

Glass, ceramic, and glass ceramic These pots are far less subject to the chemical action of foods than metals. They are breakable and heavy. No seaming makes them easy to clean. They heat slowly and unevenly, but once heated, retain the heat well. Many of them have detachable handles so that they can be used in the oven, as well as for top-stove cooking, and can also be used as serving bowls at the table.

Non-stick resin finishes These pots and pans have been improved since first introduced. The material is inert, but it must not be scratched or exposed to high heat. Either non-scratching wooden or plastic spatulas and other tools should be used with these utensils. Although adverse reports have been circulated, upon investigation the data is found to be unrelated to kitchen experiences. These pots and pans eliminate the need for oil or fat, a factor that may be of interest to those on restricted low-fat diets.

Pressure cookers Some models are available in stainless steel, as well as in aluminium. If these are used at all, the cook needs to pay scrupulously close attention to exact timing, especially for vegetables, in order to avoid overcooking and destruction of valuable nutrients. Safety features should also be carefully observed.

Stainless steel These pots and pans have lasting good appearance and superior scratch resistance. However, stainless steel is a poor heat conductor, and pots and pans made of this material do not heat evenly. For this reason other metals, such as aluminium, copper, carbon steel, or iron, are often laminated to the bottom of stainless-steel pots to distribute heat more evenly for top-stove cooking. If these pots are in long-time use, constant scouring may produce nicks that expose the other metals. If this happens, the pots should be discarded.

For those who already have a kitchen full of pots and pans the above information should serve as a checklist for gradual modifications. Don't immediately throw out all your pots and pans if, for example, they happen to be made of aluminium. Just be sure that you discontinue cooking or storing foods or beverages in them that contain acids, alkalines, or salt.* Replace them gradually with pots and pans made of more desirable materials, without straining your budget.

* What's left? Very little! You can use discarded aluminium pans as water evaporators on room radiators or as drip pans under flowerpots.

How do you adjust your favourite recipe?

By substituting certain ingredients in traditional recipes you can improve them nutritionally. Begin with your favourite recipes. Go through the listing of ingredients, and decide what substitutions they require. Try them, and make notes of what you have done. If you are not satisfied with the results on the first try, don't be discouraged. Try again with slight variations. Work at it until you are satisfied. Then note the substitutions and the amounts directly in your cookery book or on your file card. Once you have done this, you'll have the recipes permanently adjusted. Use the following guides.

Flour If your recipe calls for 1 cup of flour, 1 cup of white flour, or 1 cup of enriched white flour, substitute any of the following:

1 cup of unbleached white flour
1 cup of Cornell Mix (see p. 101)
¾ cup 100 per cent wholemeal flour
¾ to 1 cup of 81 per cent wholemeal flour

If your recipe calls for white flour in a standard recipe for yeast-raised bread, substitute an equal number of cupfuls in which you use a proportion of ¾ cup of whole wheat flour to ¼ cup of wheat germ.

If your recipe calls for white flour in a standard recipe for pie crusts, biscuits, or cakes, substitute an equal number of cupfuls in which you use a proportion of $\frac{1}{2}$ cup of whole wheat pastry flour to $\frac{1}{2}$ cup of rice flour.

If your recipe calls for white flour in a standard quick-bread recipe, such as waffles, pancakes, or muffins, substitute an equal number of cupfuls in which you use a proportion of $\frac{1}{2}$ cup of unbleached flour to $\frac{1}{2}$ cup of whole wheat flour; or $\frac{3}{4}$ cup of unbleached flour to $\frac{1}{4}$ cup of any of the following flours: corn, rice, or soy.

If you are adventurous you will want to try flours other than or in addition to wheat. The finished products may be somewhat different in taste, texture, and lightness, or heaviness. Try some replacements, and experiment until you find the combinations that you and your family enjoy. For each cup of white flour, you can substitute:

$\frac{1}{2}$ cup arrowroot flour

$\frac{1}{2}$ cup barley flour

$\frac{1}{2}$ cup cornstarch

$\frac{5}{8}$ cup potato flour

$\frac{3}{4}$ cup buckwheat flour

$\frac{3}{4}$ cup coarse cornmeal

$\frac{3}{4}$ cup oat flour

$\frac{3}{4}$ cup soy flour

$\frac{3}{4}$ to $\frac{7}{8}$ cup rice flour

$\frac{3}{4}$ cup rolled oats and $\frac{1}{4}$ cup gluten flour

$\frac{3}{4}$ to 1 cup rye flour

1 scant cup fine cornmeal

1 cup rye meal

1 cup corn flour

$1\frac{1}{3}$ to $1\frac{1}{2}$ cups rolled oatmeal

$\frac{1}{3}$ cup gluten flour and $\frac{2}{3}$ cup whole wheat flour

$\frac{1}{3}$ cup potato flour and $\frac{2}{3}$ cup rye flour

$\frac{1}{2}$ cup potato flour and $\frac{1}{2}$ cup soy flour

$\frac{5}{8}$ cup rice flour and $\frac{1}{4}$ cup rye flour

1 cup soy flour and $\frac{1}{4}$ cup potato flour

$\frac{7}{8}$ cup whole wheat flour and $\frac{1}{4}$ cup sunflower seed meal

You may wish to experiment with bean flours other than soy. They contain more protein than the grain flours, but they must be used sparingly to avoid a 'beany' flavour or very heavy texture. Grind dry beans, such as lima, pinto, navy, kidney, pea, chick pea, or lentils, in an electric blender until they are very fine in texture. Use the bean flour with whole wheat, in the proportions of four to five parts wheat to one part bean flour.

If you try combinations of flours, sift them together so that they are well mixed. Allow 10 to 20 minutes additional baking time for flours other than wheat. Lower the baking temperature (from 350° F to 325° F, 177° C to 165° C, gas mark 4–3, for example.)

Thickeners For each dessertspoon of white flour used as a thickener substitute ⅓ teaspoon of any of the following flours: arrowroot, potato, or tapioca. Before adding these thickening agents to gravies dissolve the flours in cold water. An electric blender simplifies this operation and avoids lumping. Better still, gradually wean your family away from gravies. However, these thickeners can be used validly in soufflés or custard-type desserts.

For each dessertspoon or packet of sweetened, flavoured, coloured gelatin ready-mix dessert substitute 1 dessertspoon or packet of unsweetened, plain gelatin, plus a pint of unsweetened fruit juice. Add raw fruit for extra nourishment. Or dissolve the plain gelatin in tomato or mixed vegetable juice to make aspic, and add bits of raw vegetables for extra nourishment. If you prefer to use agar-agar instead of gelatin, substitute 1 dessertspoon of agar-agar for 1 dessertspoon of gelatin, add a pint of liquid for a soft-consistency dish, or 2 dessertspoons of agar-agar for a firm consistency.

Grains If your recipe calls for a cup of uncooked white rice, substitute a cup of uncooked brown rice or ⅔ cup of any of the following uncooked grains: barley, buckwheat, or millet.

Sweeteners If your recipe calls for 1 cup of white sugar, substitute ¾ cup of honey, and reduce the milk, water, or other liquid in the recipe by ¼ cup. This is necessary because honey contains liquid. If the recipe does not contain liquid, add 4 dessertspoons of additional flour for each ¾ cup of honey used.

The moisture in honey will soften biscuit batters. This is a favourable feature if the biscuit is a soft, chewy type. However, if it is a crisp variety, add 4 extra dessertspoons of flour for each ¾ cup of honey used.

Honey caramelizes at a low temperature. Take this into account by baking with a lower oven temperature for cakes or other baked products made with honey. Otherwise they may brown outside before they are sufficiently baked inside.

Honey can replace all of the sugar used in canning, preserving, and jelly-making. An all-honey syrup is somewhat darker than a sugar syrup and tends to darken peaches and pears when they are canned. However, the honey intensifies the original fruit flavour. If you use honey to can or preserve, there are two precautions. First, since honey has a tendency to foam considerably when it is heated, there is some danger of boiling over at the beginning of the cooking period. The cooking syrup must be watched carefully. Use a large saucepan. Second, since honey is part water, it is necessary to cook the product in which honey has been used slightly longer than usual to get a specified consistency.

For honey syrups use the following proportions: 2 cups of honey to 3¾ cups of water for tart cherries, plums, apples, and strawberries; 1 cup of honey to 2 cups of water for pineapples, raspberries, peaches, sweet black cherries, and blackberries.

To make preserves with honey, follow your favourite recipes and substitute honey for the sugar. The honey will combine well with flavourings apt to be found in preserves, such as allspice, nutmeg, mace, cinnamon, cloves, and lemon or orange juice.

For jelly-making with honey, use the strong-flavoured juices, high in acid and pectin, such as tart apples, crab apples, cranberries, currants, grapes, plums, and quinces. To each cup of fruit juice add ¾ cup of honey. Cook rapidly to the usual jelly consistency. This may take slightly longer than it does when sugar is used, because the moisture in the honey must be evaporated. Remove any scum, pour into hot, sterilized glasses, and seal with paraffin.

Instead of honey you might wish to use other natural sweeteners as sugar substitutes. In any recipe that calls for 1 cup of white sugar, use instead 1 cup of black treacle or ¾ cup of black treacle and ¼ cup of blackstrap molasses. Reduce the liquid in the recipe, following the same rule as with honey. Blackstrap molasses is quite bitter. It is more palatable when it is combined with black treacle, honey, or other natural sweeteners.

A cup of white sugar can be replaced by 1¼ to 1½ cups of maple syrup, carob syrup, or malt syrup. These syrups are not quite as sweet as some others.

One cup of firmly packed brown sugar can be replaced by 1 cup of firmly packed raw sugar.

Gradually wean your family away from large amounts of concentrated sweeteners, even the natural ones. Reduce the amount of sweeteners used over foods and in home-baked items. Substitute more fresh fruits.

Dairy products For 1 cup of fresh fluid milk in any recipe you can substitute 1 cup of fresh fluid skim milk, or 3 rounded dessertspoons of non-fat dry milk powder mixed with the other dry ingredients,* plus 1 measuring cup of water, milk, or other liquid. You can add 2 teaspoonfuls of a mild-flavoured salad

* Although non-fat dry milk powder is useful as a fortifier, it should not be regarded as an equivalent of fresh fluid milk. The non-fat dry milk is relatively low in essential fatty acids and high in added synthetic vitamin D. This combination, warned Dr Hugh Sinclair of Oxford University, may lead to the wrong use of calcium in the infant's body. Many other professionals consider non-fat dry milk powder an unbalanced food, especially for infant feeding formulas.

oil, such as safflower, sesame, or sunflower, to the fresh fluid skim milk. The unsaturated oil replaces the saturated butterfat that has been removed.

For 1 cup of fresh fluid milk in any recipe you can substitute 1 cup of fluid soy milk. Soy milk has a strong flavour that is not palatable for most people. It can be somewhat disguised by molasses or honey. To reconstitute dry soy milk powder easily, dissolve it in liquid in an electric blender. If it is being used in a batter or dough, simply mix it with the dry ingredients.

For 1 cup of sour cream in any recipe you can substitute 1 cup of yogurt or buttermilk.

For 1 cup of margarine you can substitute 1 cup of butter. For 1 cup of butter or other solid shortenings you can substitute ⅔ cup of unrefined vegetable oil. For baking, use mild-flavoured oils, such as peanut, safflower, sesame, or sunflower. For table use, blend 1 cup of soft butter with ⅓ cup of mild-flavoured vegetable oil. Pat this mixture into a small bowl, refrigerate to harden, and use it as a butter spread at the table. This mixture will help reduce your family's total intake of saturated fats.

You can substitute 1 cup of unrefined vegetable oil for 1 cup of refined vegetable oil.

When you have become accustomed to using oil for cooking instead of butter, margarine, or solid shortening, you will realize that oil is easier to handle for measuring, as well as beneficial in reducing your total intake of saturates. Measure oil before you measure honey or other sweeteners in the same cup. The oil, having coated the cup, will permit all of the syrupy sweetener to leave the cup easily without any being wasted.

Seasonings For each teaspoon of salt called for in any recipe you can use a teaspoon of any of the following: sea salt, vegetable salt, or ground kelp. Better still, cut the measure in half and gradually wean your family away from salt by reducing it to a bare minimum. Finally, try to omit it entirely from food preparation. Fill your salt shakers with kelp, and let your family use this as a seasoning at the table.

Try substituting fresh or dried herbs for salt. Remember that fresh are usually stronger than dried, so use them sparingly. If you wish to preserve herbs for winter use, see p. 115.

Flavouring agents If your recipe calls for 1 square or 1 ounce of bitter chocolate, substitute 3 dessertspoons of carob powder, plus a dessertspoon each of milk (or water) and vegetable oil. Since carob is naturally sweet, you may ultimately wish to reduce the other sweetening ingredients in the recipe. If your recipe calls for 3 dessertspoons of cocoa powder, substitute 4 dessertspoons of carob powder, plus 1 dessertspoon of oil. Follow the same suggestion, given above, regarding the reduction of other sweetening ingredients in the recipe.

If your recipe calls for 1 teaspoon of vanillin, substitute 1 teaspoon of pure vanilla extract. Avoid artificial flavourings such as vanillin. They are apt to contain questionable ingredients. For example, synthetic vanilla may contain creosote and lignin, a by-product of wood pulp. Some commercial vanilla may also contain ingredients that should be avoided, such as propylene glycol, sugar, glycerin and added colour. If you cannot find a pure vanilla extract, you may wish to make your own. (See p. 117.) For variety, try combining different extracts. For example, a favourite Viennese combination is 2 parts of pure vanilla extract to 1 part of pure almond extract.

Binders and extenders If a recipe calls for 1 cup of bread-crumbs, you can substitute any of the following:

1 cup of wholemeal breadcrumbs
1 cup of wheat germ, and one raw egg
½ cup of wheat germ, ½ cup of wholemeal breadcrumbs, and
   1 raw egg

Breaders If a recipe calls for 1 cup of breadcrumbs to coat food before cooking, substitute ¼ cup each of wholemeal breadcrumbs, chopped nuts, wheat germ or medium oatmeal. Better still, wean your family away from fried foods. Bake, grill or roast instead.

Leaveners There are three different kinds of baking powder, and each one acts differently. Learn the differences. Tartaric acid baking powder reacts quickly and begins its action, even at room temperature, as soon as liquid is added to it. Phosphate baking powder acts more slowly. It requires heat to initiate its leavening action. Despite its name, double-acting baking powder reacts most slowly of all. It releases only about a third of its leavening action in the cold batter, and about two-thirds in the heat of baking. Some baking powders contain aluminium compounds, which are best avoided. If you would like to make your own baking powder, see p. 105.

Bicarbonate of soda is used alone or in combination with baking powder to leaven baked goods made with buttermilk, sour milk, yogurt, molasses, or fruit juices. The acidity of these ingredients reacts with the soda to initiate its leavening action. Once bicarbonate of soda has been put into batter, the baking should not be delayed.

If your recipe calls for 1 teaspoon of standard or double-acting baking powder, you can substitute 1 teaspoon of baking powder made without aluminium compounds. Such baking powders can be purchased at health food stores or through mail-order catalogues. Generally they contain cornstarch, bicarbonate of soda, and sodium acid pyrophosphate.

You can safely omit baking powder from almost all biscuit recipes. Wean your family away from baking powder and bicarbonate of soda, and learn to make use of any of the following healthful leaveners: baking yeast, sourdough starter, liquid yeast, or farmer's yeast (see p. 106).

Fortifiers How can I work brewer's yeast into recipes? This is a commonly asked question. Brewer's yeast can be added to a number of dishes without having members of your family revolt, because they need not even be aware of its presence. At first select only those dishes that have strong flavours. They will disguise the taste of the brewer's yeast. Use brewer's yeast in soups and stews; you will find that it actually adds good flavour to these dishes. Stir in a teaspoon of brewer's yeast for each measuring cup of soup or stew, and add it just before you are ready to serve. Make certain that it is well dissolved. The flake form dissolves more readily than the powder. Later try adding brewer's yeast in the following amounts to any of these dishes:

1 dessertspoon, to a standard pancake or waffle batter, recipe for six

2 dessertspoons, in a cheese soufflé or fondue, recipe for six

2 dessertspoons, in a pumpkin pie

3 dessertspoons, in bread dough for each average-size loaf

3 dessertspoons, in each cup of baked beans

3 dessertspoons, in liver paste, recipe for six

$\frac{1}{4}$ cup, in liver loaf, recipe for six

$\frac{1}{4}$ cup, in beefburgers, meat loaf, or stuffed peppers, recipe for six

$\frac{1}{4}$ cup, in dough for gingersnaps, recipe for five dozen

$\frac{1}{3}$ cup, in standard gingerbread or Boston brown bread recipe

$\frac{1}{2}$ cup, in dough for old-fashioned molasses drop biscuits, recipe for five dozen

$\frac{1}{2}$ cup, in one pound of old-fashioned peanut butter

Are you interested in using bone-meal powder as a fortifier in foods? It can be incorporated as follows:

$\frac{2}{3}$ teaspoon in each glass of milk drink

1 teaspoon in bread dough for each average-size loaf

2 teaspoons in each pound of meat for patties or meat loaf

2 teaspoons in a standard pudding or frozen-dessert recipe for six

Bone-meal powder can also be mixed with homemade confections. Use 1 teaspoon of it for each cup of nutmeats or dried fruit. Also, it can be blended into peanut butter, in the proportion of 1 dessertspoon of bone-meal powder to 1 pound of peanut butter.

As you continue to experiment with natural foods you'll discover other substitutions and fortifications. Natural foods offer the interested housewife an expanded world of creative cookery. The novice may think that natural foods limit one's choices. On the contrary, there can be great variety as well as eating pleasure.

Do your own thing

There may be times when you simply cannot locate a certain food item or you prefer a homemade version of a commercially processed one. 'Do your own thing' is not a new phrase. It was coined more than a century ago by Emerson. Do your own thing by preparing at home some of the food items usually bought ready-made. Some will require but little time, effort, or money. In each instance you will have to decide if you really want to do your own thing.

SPROUTS

How would you like to harvest a crop of crisp vegetables every day of the year without any backbending labour, weeding, or anxiety about weather or insect pests? You can do this kind of simple gardening in your own kitchen, without any special apparatus. It requires only a few minutes a day and a few pennies of investment.

Buy any whole dried beans, seeds, peas, or grains packaged for human consumption. These include alfalfa, fenugreek, lentils, green peas, mung (or moong) beans, soybeans, and whole wheat berries, among others. Some, such as whole dried peas and lentils, are available in supermarkets; others can be found in health food stores and in the many Indian or Chinese grocers where you can often find many other beans, such as urid and moth. Do not use seeds intended for planting purposes, since they may have been treated with poisons. Do not eat potato sprouts since they are toxic.

Among many containers used for sprouting I've seen the following used successfully: unglazed flowerpots, colanders, triangular sink strainers, tea strainers, coffee percolators, terry-cloth towels, sponges, blotting paper, and commercial sprouters. In my experience the easiest and simplest apparatus is an ordinary wide-mouthed pint-, quart-, or two-quart glass jar. Place a dessertspoon of seeds in the pint-size jar, and proportionate amounts in the larger jars. Fill the jar half full with lukewarm water. Cut two six-inch squares of nylon netting (approximately $\frac{1}{4}$-inch-hole mesh), and place the squares over the top of the jar, securing them with two rubber bands. Allow the seeds to soak overnight.

In the morning leave the netting intact, but allow the water to drain out of the jar. Then place the jar directly under the tap and allow lukewarm water to fill the jar through the netting. Shake the jar with a rotary motion to rinse the seeds, and tip the jar, allowing the water to drain out through the netting. Gently shake out any excess water, and, if possible, allow the jar to stand inverted in a dish-drainer.

In the evening rinse the seeds in the same way. Repeat the rinsings morning and evening for the next three or four days. Always make certain that the seeds are kept moist, but not standing in water. If they are not kept moist, they will dry out; if they stand in water, they will rot.

By the third or fourth day, depending on the size of the seeds and the room temperature, the sprouts should be ready to eat. Alfalfa, red clover, and fenugreek sprouts are ready when they are one to two inches long; moong (or mung) beans, one and one and a half inches long; lentils, peas, and radish sprouts, one inch long; and wheat berry sprouts, a quarter to a half inch long.

In my kitchen there are three glass jars of sprouts growing every day of the year. Each day a new one is begun, and every third day one is ready. By rotating, I 'harvest' a daily crop. My favourites? Top choices go to alfalfa for flavour; fenugreek for crispness; and mung beans for ease of sprouting. Although

I think that red clover is on a par with alfalfa, it is more difficult to find. And soybean sprouts, though highly nourishing and good-tasting, require special care to prevent moulding or rotting. I advise beginners to try mung beans first. Wheat berries sprout readily, but if they are allowed to sprout too long, they become matted, tough, and unpalatable for most people. Radish seeds are tangy and pleasant for occasional fare, but not for frequent eating. Try a variety of seeds and discover those that please you and your family most.

Although a variety of materials can be used to cover the jar, such as stainless-steel wire mesh, cheesecloth, gauze, or pieces of stocking or curtain, I prefer the nylon netting. It does not stain or discolour readily. The same squares can be used repeatedly for several months. Two layers are better than one, as the tiny alfalfa seeds, before swelling and sprouting, can slip through a single layer during the rinse. The *two* rubber bands act as a safety measure, in the same way that a man wears a belt *and* a pair of braces to hold up his trousers! You can use string or wire instead of the rubber bands.

There are two schools of thought as to whether growing sprouts should be placed in a dark cupboard or exposed to light. The former location helps develop more vitamin C, but the latter develops more chlorophyll and better flavour. I prefer to sprout my seeds in light, but not in direct sunlight. Since sprouts are not an especially high or dependable source of vitamin C, I favour the chlorophyll and flavour factors, especially with alfalfa sprouts. However, soybean sprouts do better in the dark. A few words of caution: never eat potato sprouts, which are poisonous.

Use sprouts as soon as they are ready. They are best served raw. If you do not plan to use them immediately, refrigerate them as you would any fresh vegetable and use them within a day of two. If they begin to turn brown, regard them as a wilted vegetable declining in food value.

How do you eat sprouts? Add them to a tossed mixed salad. If the sprouts are delicate, such as alfalfa or red clover,

7

use them as a garnish on the salad *after* you have tossed it with dressing. This prevents these particular sprouts from going limp. It is not necessary to do this with fenugreek or mung beans, since they retain their crispness even after being marinated with dressing.

You can make interesting raw relishes with sprouts. Mix them with diced tomato, green pepper, onion, or pimento, and add a tangy dressing.

Blend sprouts into sandwich spreads or use them in sandwiches instead of lettuce. Press them into the spread so that they don't fall out. Do *not* cut the sandwich in half.

Use sprouts as garnishes over soups, casseroles, stews, or scrambled eggs, just before serving.

Blend raw sprouts into fruit or vegetable juices in an electric blender.

Garnish a bowl of breakfast cereal and yogurt or a fresh fruit salad with sprouts.

HOMEMADE SALAD DRESSING

It is easy to make your own salad dressing if you have an electric blender. Since you will be serving large salads twice a day, and using quite a bit of dressing, here is a basic dressing that provides an excellent way of including yogurt without anyone being aware of its presence. If some members of your family think that they loathe yogurt, try this dressing and see what happens. Measure into the container of your food blender 1 cup of yogurt and $\frac{1}{2}$ cup each of vegetable oil and apple-cider vinegar. Blend thoroughly.

There are also many variations on this basic dressing. You can add garlic, pimento, herbs, kelp, or whatever you usually enjoy in salad dressing.

BREAKFAST CEREAL

If your family enjoys a dry breakfast cereal, you can mix your own and make a nutritious blend. This is a popular one, and can be adapted with many variations. In a large mixing bowl place 3 pounds of rolled oats; 1 pound each of raw sunflower, pumpkin and sesame seeds; 1 pound of raw peanuts; ½ pound each of unsweetened coconut shreds and soya flour; ½ pound each of cut-up pitted dates, figs, raisins, and dried apricots. Blend thoroughly and store in tightly closed containers. Keep it cool and dry. Refrigerate it in hot weather. When you are ready to serve this mixture, add wheat germ, ground flaxseed (optional), yogurt, and fresh fruit. If your family prefers a cereal that is less coarse in texture, all of the seeds and nuts can be ground before the dried fruit is added.

CORNELL MIX BREAD

This bread, developed by Dr Clive M. McCay and his associates at Cornell University, is also known as Cornell Triple-Rich Bread and High Protein Bread. If your family has been accustomed to eating ordinary white bread, you can convert them to eating this bread, since its appearance is similar: its taste and nutritiousness are superior.

This is the Cornell formula: for each cup of flour, first place in the measuring cup 1 dessertspoon each of soya flour and non-fat dry-milk powder, as well as 1 teaspoonful of wheat germ. Then fill the remainder of the cup with unbleached or 81 per cent wholemeal flour. This blend can be mixed easily at home. The formula works well with any recipe that calls for white flour.

BREAD RECIPE USING CORNELL MIX

I have made slight modifications in the original recipe. It will make three moderate-sized loaves.

Measure 3 cups of warm water (85° F, or 30° C) into a large bowl. Add 2 dessertspoons of dry yeast granules (or 2 packets of yeast, or 2 squares of yeast) and 2 dessertspoons of honey. Stir and allow the mixture to stand for five minutes.

By now the yeast mixture should be frothy. Stir into it 1 dessertspoon of sea salt, earth salt, or kelp, or a mixture of any of these three seasonings. Add half of the flour mixture. Beat it vigorously, using about seventy-five strokes by hand or for two minutes if you are using an electric mixer.

Add 2 dessertspoons of vegetable oil and the remainder of the flour mixture. Blend all of the ingredients thoroughly, and turn the dough out onto a floured board. Have additional flour handy, since more may be needed. Knead vigorously for about five minutes until the dough is smooth and elastic. Place it in an oiled bowl, oil the top of the dough lightly, and cover the bowl. Place it in a warm place (80° F–85° F, or 26° C–30° C) until it is nearly double in size. This will take about forty-five minutes.

Punch down the dough, fold over the edges, and turn it upside down in the bowl to rise another twenty minutes.

Turn the dough onto the board, and divide it into three portions. Fold each one inward, and form smooth, tight balls. Cover them with a clean cloth and allow them to rest ten minutes.

Shape into three loaves, or two loaves and a pan of rolls. Place in buttered tins ($3\frac{1}{2} \times 7\frac{1}{2}$ inches). Allow the dough to rise in the tins until it is doubled in bulk. This will take about forty-five minutes. Bake in a pre-heated moderate oven (350° F or 176° C, gas mark 3–4) for about fifty minutes. If the loaves begin to turn brown in fifteen to twenty minutes, reduce the temperature to 325° F or 165° C. Soya flour browns baked goods more rapidly.

Remove the finished breads or rolls from the pans and cool them on racks. If desired, brush the tops with melted butter.

100 PER CENT WHOLE WHEAT BREAD, NO KNEADING

If you can wean your family away from white bread, you may

arrive at the point where you want to try a whole wheat recipe. The following one is so quick and easy to follow, even for a novice, that it never fails. It is a recipe that I have worked out over the years to demonstrate before women's clubs. Since the recipe requires no kneading and can be done so quickly, I find that many women who have seen it demonstrated go home and make bread. I have met some of them years later, and they tell me that they are still making bread with this recipe. The recipe has spread to young men and women living in the universities, to high school students interested in natural foods, and has even been successfully made by kindergarten children, aided by teachers. Would you like to try it? The recipe makes six medium-size loaves.

Pour 3 cups of warm water into a small bowl. Add 1 dessertspoon, 1 packet, or 1 square of dried yeast. Stir. Add 2 dessertspoons of honey or unsulphured molasses. Allow the mixture to rise and bubble for about ten minutes.

Meanwhile, in a large bowl, measure 14 cups ($4\frac{1}{2}$ pounds) of unsifted freshly ground 100 per cent wholemeal compost-grown flour and 1 dessertspoon of sea salt, earth salt, kelp, or a mixture of them.

When the yeast-water-honey mixture bubbles, pour it into the flour-salt mixture. Mix thoroughly with your hands, adding about 3 to $3\frac{1}{2}$ cups of additional warm water. The dough should be firm, like the consistency of modelling clay. When it is thoroughly mixed, it should form a mass, and the bowl should appear clean. If the dough is too thin, add a little more flour; if too thick, add a little more water. The recipe is not fussy, and the proportions do not have to be exact. When the dough is the right consistency, pat it down in the bottom of a bowl. Flatten the surface, and seal off all cracks in the top. You can do this easily by putting some cold water on your fingertips. The dough should only come halfway up the side of the bowl. Pour about 1 dessertspoon of vegetable oil over the top of the dough, and pat it over the surface. This will prevent any hard crust from forming. Cover the bowl and place it in a warm place, away from draughts, for two to three hours, depending on the room temperature, until the dough has doubled in bulk and risen to the top of the bowl.

Divide the dough into six equal portions. Simply shape it into loaves, without any kneading. Slip each portion into a buttered bread pan ($3\frac{1}{2} \times 7\frac{1}{2}$ inches). Place all six bread pans *immediately* on the middle oven rack, with air spaces around the pans if possible, and set the oven temperature at 325° F to 350° F (165° C to 176° C, gas mark 3–4), depending on your oven. Note that you have allowed no rising time. The dough will rise somewhat in the oven. Note, also, that you are baking the bread in an oven that has *not* been preheated. I find that the tops of the loaves develop fewer cracks this way.

Set your kitchen timer clock for fifty minutes, and check your breads. In some ovens they may need another ten minutes. When they are golden brown and crusty, turn them out of the bread pans onto cooling racks.

This bread recipe can be doubled and still made with ease. Simply measure the ingredients for six loaves into one large bowl, and for six into another bowl. Bake all twelve loaves together. The recipe can be divided in half or in thirds to make two or three loaves.

If you do not have a large mixing bowl, use an inexpensive enamelware canning saucepan. If your sink is large enough so that you can place your mixing bowl in it, you will find that the working level is good for mixing the dough by hand. If your mixing bowl is too large to fit into the sink recess, elevate yourself by standing on a footstool and work at a table.

Consider this recipe as a basic one. Experiment with other whole grain flours to replace the wheat in part. Add brewer's yeast, bone meal, rice polish, or other fortifiers. Replace part of the water with egg: one egg for each loaf makes a good-tasting, nutritious bread. Add celery, dill, or caraway seeds to the dough for different flavours. Replace part of the flour with pumpkin-seed or sunflower-seed meal. Add raisins dipped in flour, or other dried fruit cut into small pieces.

GRINDING YOUR OWN GRAIN

If you arrive at the point of using whole grains and bypassing white flour, even the unbleached type, you will realize the importance of freshly ground whole grain flour and cereal. Ultimately the most satisfactory way of making certain that the grain is fresh is to have it ground to order. Perhaps you can convince some enterprising store-keeper – a supermarket, Co-op, neighbourhood grocer, or health food store – to invest in a stone-grinding mill. If you are prepared to wait a few minutes to have freshly ground coffee, why not follow the same procedure for flour or cereal?

If you fail to interest any of these groups, perhaps you can organize a group of organic gardeners to share the cost, along with its efforts in arranging for group orders and swaps. If costs are shared by a number of families, I suspect that within a few years the initial investment of a stone-grinding mill will have paid for itself. Substantial savings can be realized from purchases of whole grains in hundred-pound sacks. If the grain is clean, and stored in tightly closed containers in a cool, dry place, it keeps well without refrigeration.

HOMEMADE BAKING POWDER

Would you like to make your own sodium-free baking powder? Mix together 2 cups each of arrowroot flour and cream of tartar. Add 1 cup of potassium bicarbonate, which you can buy from a chemist. Sift all the ingredients together, and store the mixture in a tightly closed jar. Keep it cool and dry. Before using it, sift. Use this mixture in the same proportions as commercial baking powder.

HOMEMADE SOURDOUGH STARTER

Sourdough starter, to make a traditional American style loaf, with good nutritional value, can be made simply by reserving a cup or two of batter or dough before the remainder is cooked or baked. It is preferable to use batter or dough without salt and before bread dough is punched down or kneaded. The bit saved should be stored in a scalded glass jar or crock, covered, and left at room temperature for several days.

You can also make your sourdough from scratch by starting with some baking yeast, water, and any whole grain flour or combination of flours. Try the following: dissolve $\frac{1}{2}$ dessertspoon of dried yeast granules, or $\frac{1}{2}$ cake of yeast, or $\frac{1}{2}$ packet of yeast in $\frac{1}{2}$ cup of lukewarm water. In ten minutes the surface should be frothy. Gradually add 1 cup of whole grain flour and an additional half cup of warm water. Beat the mixture thoroughly. Proceed as with the saved batter, by placing it in a scalded glass jar or crock. After several days it will look somewhat different from the sourdough made from reserved batter or dough. A solid mass will have settled to the bottom, while the liquid will have risen to the top. Merely stir it, and it will be ready to use.

You can add the sourdough starter to your favourite recipe for pancakes, waffles, muffins, or cake batter, or add it to bread dough. You can use the sourdough in addition to your usual leavening or use it to replace the leavening entirely or in part. Although baked products may not rise as high with sourdough as with other leaveners, they have other qualities. They contain beneficial lactic acid, and the sourdough imparts a delicate flavour to the food.

If you make this sourdough recipe and add it to a recipe for baked goods, remember that you have added a pint of ingredients not called for in the original recipe. You will need to decrease correspondingly the flour and liquid in your recipe. Also, after mixing your dough or batter with the sourdough, remember to reserve a pint of it for your next baking.

If you bake less frequently than every few days, you can slow down the souring process in the sourdough by refrigerating it. If you don't plan to use the sourdough for several weeks, freeze or dry it, and then reactivate it at a later date.

To dry sourdough, add enough flour to shape it into a ball. Place it in a bag of flour. In the dried form the yeast goes into a spore stage and remains inert for a long time. Warmth and water return the yeast to an active stage.

With care you should be able to continue your sourdough for a long time. However, if it should develop any unusual appearance or odour, discard it and start anew. As you now know, this is done easily.

HOMEMADE LIQUID YEAST

You can make other starters or ferments to be used as leaveners. Would you like to try liquid yeast? Pare and cube 3 raw, sound potatoes (about ¾ of a pound). Put them in a pot with 1¼ cups of water. Simmer until the potatoes are soft. Then purée them in their cooking water. Add ¼ cup of honey and additional water to make the mixture total 3¼ cups of liquid. Cool the mixture to lukewarm (82° F, 28° C). Meanwhile soak 1 dessertspoon of dried yeast granules, or 1 cake of yeast, or 1 packet of yeast in a cup of lukewarm water. When the yeast is frothy, combine the two mixtures. Pour this into a scalded glass or crock; cover, and keep it at room temperature for several days until it has achieved the desired sourness. Then add it to the batter or dough.

HOMEMADE FARMER'S YEAST

Simmer a cup of hops with their pollen in a quart of water.*

* If you live in the country, you can gather and dry your own wild hops. Otherwise buy them from a health store or chemist who supplies home beer-making ingredients.

Cool and strain out the hops. Return the water to the pot. Add cubes of 4 raw, sound, pared potatoes (about 1 pound). Cover the pot and simmer until the potatoes are soft. Purée the potatoes, and add ½ cup of honey. Add enough whole grain flour – traditionally barley flour is included in this mixture – to make a thick batter. Soak 2 dessertspoons of dried yeast granules, or 2 cakes of yeast, or 2 packets of yeast in ¼ cup of lukewarm water. When the yeast is frothy, add it to the batter and mix well. Pour it into a scalded glass jar or crock, cover, and proceed as with the liquid yeast.

You can add more whole grain flour to the farmer's yeast, so that the texture becomes doughlike. Then it can be rolled out, cut as thin biscuits, and air-dried in the shade. When thoroughly dry, crumble the pieces and store them in an airtight container, keep in a cool dry place, and reconstitute later. This is similar to dried yeast granules.

Another leaven, in dry powder form, is not yet available, but it is well worth while suggesting to your supplier. This leaven can be used for sourdough-type bread baking and also with hot breads. The ingredients consist of lactic acid and leaven yeast culture produced in a media of bulgaricus buttermilk, primary-grown leaven yeast culture (brewer's yeast) on cornmeal from open-pollinated corn, rye, and oat meals, barley malt, blackstrap molasses, and hops.

HOMEMADE RAW SAUERKRAUT

By now you've learned to reject foodstuffs prepared with sodium benzoate. Unfortunately this preservative is frequently used in commercially prepared sauerkraut. Both flavour and food values are destroyed in canned cooked sauerkraut, and much of it is excessively salty. If you enjoy sauerkraut, which can be delicious and nutritious, try making your own. You can avoid the preservative, the need for cooking it, and you can reduce or even exclude the salt.

Homemade sauerkraut can be made quickly and easily,

even in small batches. It can be done in a small city kitchen as easily as in the suburbs or country, and it can be made with as little as one head of cabbage. Assemble a few simple items. Rummage through your household equipment and find a bowl, pot, or other wide-mouthed container that will hold a gallon of liquid measure. Glass, well-glazed clay, or other impermeable material is suitable. Once, in a junk shop I found an inexpensive secondhand one-gallon stoneware crock and cover, ideal for the purpose. I use it solely for sauerkraut-making. If you consider looking for a similar crock, check its inside first. If the crock has been used for storage of surplus eggs in water-glass, it will have a permanent whitish stain. Reject such a crock for sauerkraut production.

Next, find a flat plate, slightly smaller in diameter than the inner surface of your container. If you plan to use a sloping bowl, measure the plate against the diameter near the top of the bowl. Then locate a few large, smooth stones, and guard them against being carried off by the children as toys. Plan to reserve the container, plate, and stones exclusively for making sauerkraut.

Depending on the size of your family, shred one or two heads of solid cabbage. Place the shredded cabbage at the bottom of the container. For each head of cabbage pulverize $\frac{1}{2}$ teaspoon each of dill, celery, and caraway seeds in an electric seed grinder or with a mortar and pestle. These seeds can be added whole, but I think that the ground seeds release more flavour. If the flavour of such seeds doesn't appeal to you, omit any or all of them. They are not essential. If you do use them, mix with three dessertspoons of sea salt, kelp, or a blend of these, for each head of cabbage. Sprinkle this blend on top of the shredded cabbage.

Pour cold water over this mixture, so that the shredded cabbage is completely covered. You will need slightly more than three pints of water for each cabbage. The liquid should reach no higher than two or three inches from the top of the container, to prevent overflow during fermentation.

Put the plate over the shredded cabbage, seasoning, and water. Press down gently, so that the liquid flows over and submerges it. Next, weight it down with the freshly scrubbed stones. Cover the container, place it in a warm room, and let nature take its course. As an extra precaution against overflow – which rarely occurs – you can place the container in an old pie plate, to catch any possible drippings.

In recent years I've invented a technique for keeping down the pieces of cabbage that occasionally float up above the plate. I cut a piece of nylon netting (see p. 98 on sprouts – use the same material and gauge) and place it on top of the packed-down shredded cabbage before putting the plate on top. The netting prevents the stray cabbage pieces from floating upward, where they are apt to rot.

Within a few days you will begin to sniff the pleasant fermentation process. Take a peek now and then. Be sure that the plate keeps the cabbage submerged under the liquid. Skim off any scum that may develop on the surface. The length of fermentation time will be determined by the room's temperature. Sometimes our sauerkraut is ready in seven days; sometimes it takes slightly longer. Toward the end, check daily.

When you're convinced that the product is well fermented, remove the stones, plate and netting. Using a slotted spoon, transfer the drained sauerkraut to your prettiest serving bowl. Strain the remaining liquid. The flavour of both the raw sauerkraut and its juice will be subtle and delicate, quite unlike commercial sauerkraut.

After your family eats its fill, the remainder can be refrigerated. Although raw, it keeps well, thanks to its natural preservative, lactic acid.

Red cabbage gives sauerkraut great eye appeal. Its juice is sparkling ruby-red and deserves to be sipped from your best crystal glasses.

After you master the art of sauerkraut preparation you may wish to experiment. Add other raw vegetables and ferment them along with the cabbage. Good additions are thinly sliced onions, carrot or turnip strips, slivers of cauliflower, or radish slices. Instead of the flavouring seeds I suggested, try juniper berries, mustard seeds, or coriander seeds.

FERMENTED MILK CULTURES

Yogurt, kefir, kumiss, tette, buttermilk, and other sourmilk products also depend on those mysterious yeasts in the air to convert milk into delicious fermented products. If you wish to make yogurt simply and inexpensively using commercially available yogurt as a starter, try the following system, which requires no special equipment. Just be sure that all materials and utensils you use are scrupulously clean.

Bring a pint of fresh milk to a near boil, and cool to luke-warm (105° F to 115° F, 40° C to 46° C). Test with a sugar thermometer if you have one. Otherwise sprinkle the milk on your wrist. In time you will be able to judge how much heat and time you will need with your stove. Then you can set your kitchen timer or alarm clock as a reminder.

When the milk has cooled sufficiently, pour two tablespoons of any good quality plain commercial yogurt into the milk, and mix it well with a wooden spoon. Pour the mixture into prewarmed glasses, cups, custard cups, or wide-mouthed preserving jars, and arrange them in a heavy, deep pot with a lid. An inexpensive enamelware preserving pan is ideal for the purpose.

Pour lukewarm water into the pot until it reaches the necks of the containers. Cover the pot and wrap a heavy towel around it to conserve the heat. Instead of the preserving pan, you could use an inexpensive styrofoam picnic hamper, which is a good insulator.

From time to time check the temperature of the water. When the water cools, ladle out some of it and replace it with hot water. This must be done carefully, without disturbing the yogurt containers. For this reason it is wise not to fill the con-

tainer full of yogurt jars, but to allow room to lower the
ladle.

After two or three hours gently tilt one yogurt jar to observe
whether or not the yogurt has started to thicken. It should be
of the consistency of heavy cream and cohere when the container is tilted slightly. If it has reached this point, remove the
yogurt from the incubator and refrigerate it. If it is still thin,
allow the jars to remain in the incubator a while longer, and
check later.

The yogurt will continue to thicken as it cools. Chill it for
several hours, or even better, overnight. Save one of the jars
of yogurt and use it as a starter for subsequent batches. If the
yogurt begins to look thin and watery, you can give it a boost
by adding more commercial yogurt.

In preparing subsequent batches you can use less yogurt as
a starter. Or you can use the same amount of yogurt starter,
with more heated milk. If you like thick yogurt, add 2 tablespoons of non-fat milk powder to the liquid milk before you
heat it.

Some people are prejudiced against yogurt without ever
having tasted it, or, having tasted some commercially prepared
product, have decided against it. If you happen to be in the
former category, try yogurt with sweet fruit, such as prunes.
Frequently people who do not like plain yogurt discover that
they do like it combined with something else. If you have only
sampled commercially prepared yogurt – sometimes a highly
contrived and modified product – by all means be willing to
try homemade yogurt. You will discover that they are dis-
tinctly different. If you don't like the tartness of yogurt, you
can control this in making homemade yogurt. You can
keep the yogurt mild by shortening the incubation period.
Refrigerate it as soon as the yogurt begins to thicken slightly.
If you prefer a tart, tangy yogurt, incubate it longer. For an
easy way to introduce the novice to yogurt, see homemade
salad dressing (p. 100) and fruit whip (p. 118).

HOMEMADE SNACKS

Some people are addicted to snacking. Family eating habits have changed to such an extent that many families no longer sit down to eat together, but snack on the run all day long. Consequently it is important to make the snacks nutritious. Here are a few suggestions.

Toasted soybeans Soak a cup of dry soybeans overnight in a quart of cold water. The next day drain the liquid. Dry the soybeans between towels. Spread them out in a shallow pan and dry them slowly (about two hours) in a low oven (200° F, 93° C). Then place them under the grill. Occasionally shake the pan. Allow the soybeans to become lightly toasted. Remove from the oven. The toasted soybeans can be eaten as they are or oiled and seasoned.

Cheese-flavoured straws Grate a pound of sharp Cheddar cheese (4 cups) and turn it into a large bowl. Add a cup of vegetable oil, 3 cups of whole grain flour, and as much nonfat milk powder as the mixture will hold. Mix it with your hands and shape it into long, flattened rolls. Wrap them in wax paper and chill. Then slice thin and bake in a preheated moderate oven (375° F, 190° C, gas mark 4) for about six minutes.

Herbed toasted coconut If you want to make a special treat for guests, try serving these as an appetizer with drinks both alcoholic and non-alcoholic. Cut a fresh coconut into bite-size pieces. Place them in a shallow baking pan and dry them slowly in a low oven (200° F, 93° C, gas mark 1). Turn them into a bowl and add a mixture of the following: ½ teaspoonful each of garlic powder, sweet paprika, kelp, mixed crushed herbs, brewer's yeast and ground cumin seed. Coat the coconut pieces with the blend and store in a tightly closed jar.

A TEENAGE PARTY TREAT

Teenagers adore pizzas. Give them a wholesome version of this popular snack. The recipe is easy and they can prepare it themselves. Mix a yeast-raised bread dough. (See Cornell Mix, p. 101, or whole grain dough, p. 102.) Pat a thin layer of dough into the bottoms of well-oiled pie plates. Allow about an hour for the dough to rise. Then arrange well-drained stewed tomatoes on top of the dough, saving the juice for soup stock. Sprinkle oregano and basil on top of the tomatoes, and add grated hard cheese. Bake the pizzas in a preheated moderate oven (350° F to 375° F, 177° C – 190° C, gas mark 3 to 4) for 20 to 30 minutes until the crust is thoroughly baked. At the last minute the pizzas can be placed under the grill to turn the cheese golden brown. Cut into wedges and serve with a large tossed salad and fresh fruit for dessert.

HOMEMADE PEANUT BUTTER

Since old-fashioned 100 per cent peanut butter has virtually disappeared from most supermarkets, except in rare instances, you might want to try making your own. The consistency will not be as fine as commercial peanut butter, but the taste is excellent. And there are none of the hydrogenated fats, added sugar, texturizers, antioxidants, and other questionable chemical additives that have insidiously crept into peanut butter, although those sold in health stores are usually fine.

Grind about $\frac{1}{4}$ cup of raw or roasted peanuts at a time in an electric blender or seed grinder. Keep emptying the contents into a bowl. If you are using a seed grinder, allow it to cool for a few minutes between grindings, in order not to overwork the motor.

When you have ground a sufficient amount of peanut meal for your needs, add a small quantity of vegetable oil, and – if you wish – a dash of sea salt, and/or kelp. Blend thoroughly with a spatula until the mass holds together. You can also add fortifiers, such as brewer's yeast, bone-meal powder, wheat germ, ground sesame seeds, rice polish, or soya flour. You can grind other nuts, instead of or in addition to the peanuts, and mix them together. If you thin the nut butter with water and blend it in the electric blender, it will be converted into a nut-milk drink.

BRINED HERBS

Certain herbs lose a great deal of flavour when they are dried. I find this to be particularly true of dill, tarragon, basil and parsley. For wintertime use, to retain the flavour of these four herbs, I put them in brine. They are not quite as good as fresh summertime herbs, but they are superior to dried. Would you like to try brining herbs?

Mince the herb while it is still fresh. Put a layer of herb at the bottom of a wide-mouthed glass jar. Strew a layer of sea salt, or powdered kelp on top. Continue by alternating layers of herb and layers of seasoning until the jar is filled. Keep pressing it down. You can pack quite a lot into a jar. Cover the jar with a screw cap and refrigerate. When you are ready to use this brined herb, place a small quantity of it in a tea strainer and rinse off the brine by running a gentle stream of cool water through it. Or use it with the brine in unseasoned soups or stews. Use it sparingly as its flavour is concentrated.

DRYING APPLES

If you have surplus apples in the autumn, or find that some are beginning to spoil, you can salvage them for later use. Wash the apples, but do not peel them. Cut away any spots or bruises. Slice the apples one-eighth inch thick, and place the pieces on cake-cooling racks. Do not overlap. Allow them to air-dry overnight at room temperature. If you have a gentle source of heat, such as a pilot light or a banked fire from a wood stove, so much the better. When the apples are leathery but not brittle they are ready to store. There must not be enough moisture in them so that, if pressed, they feel wet. Store them in tightly closed containers and keep cool and dry. If properly prepared, they have a long storage life. Eaten like this, they are delicious snacks. They can also be added to the dry cereal mix (see p. 100). They can be reconstituted in water, but this is not necessary. Pears can be dried in the same way, and are equally delicious.

HOMEMADE VINEGAR

Homemade vinegar is so easy to make that it is surprising that so few people do it. If you have surplus apples in the autumn, and juice them, can them, freeze them, dry them, or make jelly and jam with them, you are bound to have apple pomace, skins, and cores. Put all these wastes into a wide-mouthed jar or crock. Keep adding cold water so that it is covered at all times with liquid. I use several layers of nylon netting (see p. 98 for gauge) over the top of the crock and under the cover of the crock. This keeps it closed and prevents fruit flies from getting inside.

Keep the crock in a warm place. Add fresh peelings, cores, and bruised apples from time to time. The 'mother' that forms on top will gradually thicken. When the vinegar smells and tastes sufficiently strong, skim off the 'mother', strain the vinegar, bottle, and cork it. Use the 'mother' to make additional vinegar from sweet cider. The 'mother' will act as a starter.

You can make herbed vinegar by adding one closely packed cup of minced herbs such as basil, tarragon, mint, or dill, to each pint of cider vinegar. Let the herbs steep in the vinegar for two weeks, shaking the bottles each day. When the flavour tastes sufficiently strong, strain, bottle, and cork the herbed vinegar.

HOMEMADE VANILLA EXTRACT

Cut up a vanilla bean into small pieces and place them in a bowl. Pour ¼ cup of boiling water over them, cover the bowl, and allow the mixture to steep overnight. Grind the mixture in an electric blender. Strain, and return the juice to the blender. Add ½ teaspoon of liquid lecithin and a dessertspoon each of honey and vegetable oil. Blend the mixture and pour it into a bottle. Cap it tightly and store in the refrigerator. Shake it well before using. Measure the same amount as any commercial vanilla extract when you use your favourite recipe.

MOCK JAM

You can make a delectable toast spread by cutting up dried apricots into very fine pieces with a pair of scissors and soaking them for several days in honey. The mixture will look somewhat like orange marmalade.

CONFECTIONS

In a large mixing bowl blend together equal parts of carob powder, non-fat dry milk powder, and unsweetened coconut shreds. Moisten with a small quantity of milk or water, just enough to have the mass hold together. Pat it firmly into a square Pyrex baking dish, and chill it in the refrigerator. Score it into squares and serve. Or, if time permits, you can roll the mass into small balls (walnut-size) and coat them with additional coconut shreds or sesame seeds. Cut pieces of wax paper into six-inch squares. Wrap the balls individually, and freeze them. They will unfreeze within a few minutes. Since all the ingredients are naturally sweet, it is unnecessary to use additional sweeteners.

If fresh coconut is available, use the freshly grated nutmeat, and the coconut juice instead of the milk or water as a binder.

You can also add ground nuts, sunflower or pumpkin-seed meal, or whole meal breadcrumbs to the blend. The balls can be rolled in ground nuts or seeds.

JIFFY DESSERTS

If you or other members of your family are not yet ready to accept the notion that simple fresh fruits are 'desserts', learn to make a few quick ones that dress up fruit festively. Here are some suggestions.

Date flowers Allow four dates per serving. Slit them lengthwise as deeply as the pits. Remove the pits and stuff the cavities with two raw cashews or almonds. Arrange the stuffed dates on dessert dishes in the form of a flower with petals. Add a toothpick to the dish, which will look like a stem. It will serve as a handy implement for spearing the sticky dates.

Fruit whip Blend a cup of soaked dried apricots (or peaches) with a cup of yogurt in the electric blender. If you find this too tart, add a bit of honey. Turn this purée out into six small custard cups or sherbet glasses. Using an electric seed grinder, grind $\frac{1}{4}$ cup of sunflower, pumpkin, or sesame seeds into meal. Garnish the fruit whip with it. This dessert is readily accepted by people who think that they loathe yogurt.

Frozen date dessert Pit and quarter $1\frac{1}{2}$ cups of dates, using a pair of scissors to cut them. Put in an electric blender and pour $\frac{1}{2}$ cup of warm water over them. Allow them to stand for ten minutes, then blend them. Add $1\frac{1}{2}$ cups of light cream and blend again. Pour the contents into six heavy custard cups and freeze. This dessert serves six.

Now that you have learned some of the basic principles about food, you are probably well launched on a new style of eating. What once seemed strange and complex should now be familiar and simple. As you meet other novices in this new world, remember the steps you took that gradually cleared up your own bewilderment. Pass them on.

Good eating and good health to all of you!

A list of producers and suppliers of health foods is to be found in the monthly magazines, *Here's Health* and *Health for All*, obtainable from any health food store. In case of difficulty write to: The Health Food Manufacturers' Association, The Old Coach House, Southborough Road, Surbiton, Surrey, KT6 6JN, or to the National Association of Health Stores, Bank Passage, Exchange Walk, Nottingham, who will be glad to assist.

Index

Also in Unwin Paperbacks

LET'S COOK IT RIGHT
Adelle Davis

Let's Cook it Right is one of the most popular, helpful and widely praised cook-books ever published. It is dedicated to the principle that foods can be prepared to retain both flavour and nutrients. Hundreds of basic recipes for preparing every type of food are included together with many more easy-to-fix variations on them. A major emphasis is the reduction of solid fats to a minimum and an increase in the use of vegetable oils. Adelle Davis has also eliminated any ingredients likely to contain cancer-producing additives, such as those found in some colourings, preservatives, bleaches, artificial sweeteners, flavourings and dyes.

One of the very best cook-books in the world . . . it explains in detail the method of cooking which will retain the goodness of the food, as well as producing mouthwatering meals . . . if you are interested in fine health-giving gourmet food, then you must, repeat must, have a copy.'

Yoga and Health

This is not merely a book to show how delicious foods may be prepared but a book which is a necessity for the young and inexperienced no less than for older cooks who may have forgotten the principles of nutrition.'

Womans Choice

LET'S EAT RIGHT TO KEEP FIT
Adelle Davis

Let's Eat Right to Keep Fit is a practical guide to nutrition designed to bring about good health through a proper diet. Adelle Davis discusses, in detail, the 40 or more nutrients needed by the body to build health, and explains the foods that supply them in the most concentrated form. There are chapters on essential vitamins, on the importance of reducing blood cholesterol and on nature's own tranquillizer 'magnesium'. Adelle Davis includes her own specific recommendations for a balanced diet.

'An expert but very readable guide to nutrition.'

TV Times

'Adelle Davis knew how to inspire enthusiasm for wholefood living.'
She

'Boisterous, breathless, but serious minded book.'

The Observer

LET'S GET WELL
Adelle Davis

Let's Get Well explains how a well chosen diet, which provides the most needed nutrients, can repair and rebuild a sick body. A proper diet can restore health and Adelle Davis shows in simple, non-technical terms, that recuperation can be hastened by the proper selection of natural foods supplemented by vitamins. There are full medical references. Many illnesses are covered including heart attacks, ulcers, diabetes, arthritis, gout and anaemia. Adelle Davis explains the function of nutrition in disease related to the blood system, the digestion, the liver, the kidneys and the nervous system.

'An extraordinary book, advises the millions who suffer from illness how to select the best foods that contain the most needed nutrients for repairing and rebuilding a sick body written in clear, layman's terms and backed by medical references . . . should be in every home.'
Natural Food Retailer

'A good overall picture of the relationship of nutrition to health . . . highly recommended.'
Good Health